BUSHED!

An Illustrated History of
What Passionate Conservatives Have
Done to America and the World

OTHER BOOKS BY WALTER C. CLEMENS, JR.

Dynamics of International Relations: Conflict and Mutual Gain in An Era of Global Interdependence (2004, 1998)

The Baltic Transformed: Complexity Theory and European Security (2001)

America and the World, 1898-2025: Achievements, Failures, Alternative Futures (2000)

Baltic Independence and Russian Empire (1991)

Can Russia Change? (1990)

The U.S.S.R. and Global Interdependence (1978)

The Superpowers and Arms Control (1973)

The Prospects for Peace, 1973-1977 (1973)

Die Tschechoslowakei unter Husak (1970)

The Arms Race and Sino-Soviet Relations (1968)

Outer Space and Arms Control (1966)

Khrushchev and the Arms Race: Soviet Interests in Arms Control and Disarmament, 1954-1964 (co-author, 1966)

Toward a Strategy of Peace (editor, 1965)

World Perspectives on International Politics (editor, 1965)

Soviet Disarmament Policy, 1917-1963 (comp., 1965)

OTHER BOOKS BY JIM MORIN

Jim Morin's Field Guide To Birds, William Morrow & Co. 1985

Famous Cats, William Morrow & Co. 1982

Line Of Fire, University Press Of Florida, 1991

Columba! A Cartoon History Of Latin America (contributor), Potatoe Press, 1993, Chapter 8

Eyes On the President (contributor), Chronos Publishing, 1993

Finest International Political Cartoons Of Our Time (contributor), Wittyworld Press, 1993

BUSHED!

An Illustrated History of
What Passionate Conservatives Have
Done to America and the World

Walter C. Clemens, Jr.
Illustrations by Jim Morin

Outland Books

Skaneateles, New York

For information about discount purchases, please contact Outland Books at
(315) 685-8723 or www.outlandbooks.com

Published by Outland Books
Outland Communications, LLC
P. O. Box 534
25 Hannum Street
Skaneateles, New York 13152

www.outlandbooks.com

ISBN 1-932820-00-0 (cloth)
ISBN 0-9714102-5-9 (paper)

Library of Congress Cataloging-in-Publication Data
to be found at the Library of Congress

Design by Outland Books
Cover design by Denice Stowe

Printed in the United States of America

for

AMERICA AND THE WORLD

Et dimitte nobis debita nostra,
sicut et nos dimittimus debitoribus nostris.
Et ne passus nos fueris induci in tentationem,
Sed libera nos a malo.

(Matt. VI. 9-11)

BRIEF CONTENTS

Acknowledgments   xiii

Introduction: How Could So Much Go So Wrong So Quickly?   xv

1. Bad for Texas, Worse for America: Privilege Without Heart or Principle 1

2. Bushonomics: Voodoo Economics or Kleptomania?   11

3. Secrets of Energy: California Dreamin'   25

4. The Democracy Money Can Buy   43

5. Green or Black? The Weight of Big Coal and Big Oil   55

6. Mind Control: Drill and Kill   69

7. Appeals to Faith: In George We Trust?   81

8. Us and Them: How to Lose Friends and Inspire Enemies   97

9. Making the World Safe for Americans: Preempt!   109

10. Washington's Bipolar Disorders: China and Russia   125

11. "Honest Brokering" in the "Holy Land"   139

12. Jihads→Crusades→Jihads→?   149

13. To Fight Evil, Must One Do Evil?   163

14. War: Politics by Other Means   183

15. Pay-Offs: The Worst Presidency in U.S. History?   203

End Notes   225

Suggested Readings   235

Suggested Web Sites   242

DETAILED CONTENTS

Introduction: How Could So Much Go So Wrong So Quickly?   xv

1.   **Bad for Texas, Worse for America: Privilege Without Heart or Principle 1**
      - *Class Credentials*   2
      - *Super Patriot Untested*   2
      - *The Terminator*   3
      - *Finality, Pushed by Jim Crow in Cyberspace*   5
      - *The Supreme Court Decides the People's Choice*   7
      - *Sheiks and Moonies Help the Dynasty and Vice Versa*   9
      - *Just Say No*   10

2.   **Bushonomics: Voodoo Economics or Kleptomania?**   **11**
      - *Slight of Hand*   12
      - *A Magic Elixir*   12
      - *Divine Intervention?*   14
      - *Deep Pockets - Your Social Security!*   14
      - *Contributions and/or Votes Welcome*   15
      - *Safe Havens*   16
      - *Don't the Rich Deserve a Break?*   17
      - *Steel Till it Hurts*   18
      - *Why America Needs China*   19
      - *Wal-Martization*   19
      - *So How Much do Tax Cuts Costs?*   20
      - *Rules - Who Needs Them?*   23

3.   **Secrets of Energy: California Dreamin'**   **25**
      - *What You Don't Know Can't Hurt Me*   26
      - *The VP vs. Government Inspectors*   28
      - *Stonewalling Around the White House*   29
      - *The News: Enron May Have More Tax Havens Than Halliburton!*   30
      - *Unregulated Groping*   31
      - *Thermostats Set for Profits*   33
      - *Megawatt Laundering*   34
      - *"Kenny, I Hardly Knew Yuh"*   34
      - *How to Build a Nest Egg: Lessons From Enron*   35
      - *How De-Reg Can Regulate Family Ties*   36
      - *Shocked to the Pitt*   36
      - *Secrets of Horatio Alger (Make Sure Poppy is Prez)*   37
      - *Martha Stewart Before Kenneth Lay?*   38
      - *Black Marks on the White House*   39
      - *Halliburton Means Cost-Plus*   40

4.   **The Democracy Money Can Buy**   **43**
      - *Does Money Talk? 2 x 1 = Bush defeats McCain*   43
      - *Should Money Talk? The Seduction of Power*   44
      - *Caught in the Act*   45
      - *Forced to Sign, Free to Skirt*   47
      - *Hard Money as Free Speech*   48
      - *"All Power Grows From the Barrell of a Gun": Mao Zedong and the NRA*   51
      - *Subsidies for Manure Cleanup*   52
      - *Swarmy Incest*   53
      - *The Omega and Alpha of Evil*   53

5. **Green or Black? The Weight of Big Coal and Big Oil**   **55**
    - *Foxes and Lions to Guard Chickens*   *56*
    - *Full Steam*   *57*
    - *No Trees, No Fires*   *59*
    - *"D" for Disasters*   *60*
    - *Some Like it Hot*   *61*
    - *"O Beautiful for Spacious Skies"*   *62*
    - *Damn the Bureaucracy, Full Speed Ahead!*   *63*
    - *Crawford, Da; Yellowstone, Nyet*   *64*
    - *"For Purple Mountain Majesties Above the Fruited Plain!"*   *65*

6. **Mind Control: Drill and Kill**   **69**
    - *Many Children Left Behind*   *71*
    - *Reaching for Minimal Skills in Texas*   *72*
    - *Underfunded Mandates*   *72*
    - *Do Sticks Work Better Than Carrotts?*   *74*
    - *Suffer the Children*   *75*
    - *Potemkin Alternatives*   *75*
    - *Let Them Eat Cake*   *76*
    - *Musical Robots*   *77*
    - *Power of Example*   *78*
    - *Business Ethics: "Cats," Emily Dickinson or Machiavelli*   *79*

7. **Appeals to Faith: In George We Trust?**   **81**
    - *God + Government = ?*   *83*
    - *Not Just Tax Cuts But Vouchers Also Can Work Wonders*   *83*
    - *Shall We Subsidize Jihad?*   *85*
    - *And Why Not Scientology?*   *86*
    - *Safety-Locks for Columbine*   *87*
    - *Faithful Sex*   *88*
    - *Life, Liberty and Abortion*   *89*
    - *Punching Holes in the War on Condoms*   *90*
    - *Washington Left Breastless!*   *90*
    - *Faith-Constrained Science?*   *92*
    - *Some Clones Superior to Others?*   *93*
    - *When Are Executions Just? Does it Matter?*   *94*
    - *Apocalypse Now (But Donations Welcome Anyway)*   *94*

8. **Us and Them: How to Lose Friends and Inspire Enemies**   **97**
    - *Who or What Can Replace the Evil Empire?*   *98*
    - *"I Believe What I Believe is Right"*   *100*
    - *Bare Confrontations in the Old World*   *100*
    - *One Figurehead to Another*   *101*
    - *Blowback*   *102*
    - *Passionate Conservatism Twists the Knife*   *103*
    - *Nuanced Options*   *104*
    - *Britain's Most Unpopular Visitor Since 1066*   *105*
    - *How the U.S. Became Its Own Worst Enemy*   *105*
    - *Bush-Style Humility on the World Scene*   *106*

9. **Making the World Safe for Americans: Preempt!**   **109**
    - *What You Don't Know Can Hurt Somebody Else*   *112*
    - *In Bed with a Complex*   *112*
    - *Can Antimissile Missiles Stop Suitcase Bombs?*   *113*
    - *How To Rebuild the Beijing-Moscow Axis*   *115*
    - *Conservatives vs. the Law*   *116*

	- How to Shoot Yourself in the Foot in Outer Space	*117*
	- Departments of Evasion	*118*
	- Against Balkanization	*119*
	- Long After the Shooting Subsides	*120*
	- How Nukes Small and Large Can Serve U.S. Objectives	*121*
	- New Medicine From a Strange Doctor	*121*
	- Who Needs Congress if We Have a Commander-in-Chief?	*122*
	- Worst Case Worries	*123*
10.	**Washington's Bipolar Disorders: China and Russia**	**125**
	- Trade = Peace?	*126*
	- China's Bipolar Problem	*126*
	- More Than Tête-à-Tête	*127*
	- No Take-Outs Needed	*128*
	- A Loose Cannon vs. Diplomatic Ambiguity	*129*
	- Where China Takes First Place	*130*
	- A Judge of Character	*130*
	- Cold War is Passé	*131*
	- Glastnost Closing	*132*
	- Can a Lube Job Smooth Over Genocide?	*132*
	- New Found Intimacies (Machiavelli Would Smile)	*134*
	- A Meeting of Bodies But Not of Minds	*134*
	- Bush's Reward for Appeasing Beijing on Xinjiang and Taiwan	*134*
	- A Holey Alliance	*135*
	- Xenophobia + Fascism = ?	*136*
	- Xenophobia + Fascism + Antisemitism = The Presidency	*136*
11.	**"Honest Brokering" in the "Holy Land"**	**139**
	- "Perfidious Albion" Plants Seeds of Conflict	*140*
	- Whose Orange Groves? Whose State?	*141*
	- The Bush and Saudi Dynasties Enrich Each Other	*142*
	- America's Christian Zionists	*142*
	- Imbalances of Terror	*143*
	- Better Late Than Never?	*144*
	- Dialogue	*145*
	- Dictated Democracy	*146*
	- Do Walls Work?	*146*
12.	**Jihads→Crusdades→Jihads→?**	**149**
	- Other Priorities Delayed Action Against Al Qaeda	*150*
	- Why Hate Infidels?	*151*
	- Dynastic Marriages	*152*
	- Cultural Relativism: T-Shirts as Justification for Rape	*152*
	- Cultural Absolutism (Useful Hints for Texans?)	*153*
	- Afghan Warlords Better Partners Than NATO Allies?	*153*
	- The Pentagon's Revolution in Military Technology	*154*
	- Cultural Relativism on the Playing Field	*154*
	- What Will Follow Psych-Ops?	*155*
	- Afghanistan Under U.S. Tutelage: #1 in Opium	*155*
	- The U.S. Aligns with Islamic States Against Women's Rights	*156*
	- Qatar's Answer to Fox News	*156*
	- Dubya Not Wild About Harmony While Rumsfeld Demands Solo	*157*
	- Karzai Collects Millions But Needs Many Billions	*159*
	- A Long Slog Ahead, Rumsfeld Concedes	*160*
	- "God Gave us Bush," Pentagon Intelligence Chief Reveals	*161*

13.   **To Fight Evil, Must One Do Evil?**   **163**
      - *The Mayor's Presence, the President's Voice*   *164*
      - *Ask Not What You Can Do For Your County....*   *165*
      - *Denouncing Evil*   *165*
      - *A Phrase George Orwell Would Relish*   *166*
      - *Forget Osama, Let's Target Oregon!*   *167*
      - *The FBI Tunes in to the Confessional*   *167*
      - *Courts, "No"; Gitmo, "Sí"*   *169*
      - *The NRA Trumps the FBI*   *170*
      - *Dubya and Enron Get a Nearly Free Ride*   *171*
      - *Homeland Security @ $25 Million = Color Coded Alerts*   *171*
      - *The Benefits of Privatization*   *173*
      - *Big Brother vs. Whistle-Blowers*   *174*
      - *Centralized Security Omits the Three Most Important Agencies*   *176*
      - *Another Enemy Combatant?*   *178*
      - *1984 Arrives Two Decades Late*   *178*
      - *Be Afraid...and Do As You're Told*   *180*

14.   **War: Politics by Other Means**   **183**
      - *The Passionate Quest of Passionate Conservatives*   *184*
      - *A Hedged Estimate Twisted Into a Rationale for War*   *184*
      - *Blair Joins the Ministry of Untruth*   *187*
      - *A Dangerous Doctrine Confuses Long-Term with Immediate Threats*   *188*
      - *What's the Rush?*   *189*
      - *War as the Continuation of Politics*   *190*
      - *Why So Tough on Baghdad But not Pyongyang?*   *191*
      - *Let Them Hate us so Long as They Fear us*   *192*
      - *Dissent = Unpatriotic ?*   *193*
      - *An Unholy Alliance*   *193*
      - *America Deceived by Wishful Thinking and Hubris*   *194*
      - *White House Treason*   *195*
      - *Disinformed and Deluded*   *197*
      - *A Balance Sheet: Saddam Gone, But at What Price?*   *199*

15.   **Pay-Offs: The Worst Presidency in U.S. History?**   **203**
      - *Morality*   *203*
      - *Spirit and the National Agenda*   *205*
      - *Glaucon's Ring at Work*   *207*
      - *Pay-Offs for Passionate Conservatives*   *207*
      - *Waste Not, Want Not?*   *209*
      - *The Democracy Money Can Buy*   *210*
      - *Administrative Efficiency*   *211*
      - *America's Threat to the Biosphere*   *212*
      - *Mind Control, Drill and Kill*   *214*
      - *The First Amendment*   *216*
      - *How to Lose Friends and Inspire Enemies*   *217*
      - *Has the War on Terrorism Improved American Security?*   *219*
      - *Balance Sheet: Performance Within The Context of the Times*   *222*

Acknowledgments

My first debt is to the late Soviet Union, where I lived and studied for a time, for cultivating an allergy to self-righteous dogmatism, deception, and manipulation in the quest for power by a clutch of unworthies who did far more harm than good for their society.

An incisive image is worth thousands of words. Jim Morin's cartoons, conceived in real time as key events took shape over the past four years, tell us a great deal about how President George W. Bush and his team tried to steer the United States and the world. My commentary recalls the time and place of those key events, trying to put them in historical context. The analysis also evaluates the impact of the Bush team's policies. Whose interests did these policies serve? To what extent did they succeed or fall short? The stakes are so immense that a sober assessment is due now. In time, additional discoveries will emerge from classified archives and various undisclosed locations. New revelations and insights will compel some rethinking, but the main trends are already clear.

Most of the publications and Web sites that buttressed this study are listed in the endnotes and select bibliography. Columns by Paul Krugman, Bob Herbert, Maureen Dowd, and Nicholas Kristoff in *The New York Times* triggered much of the analysis. Many issues have come into focus for me thanks to in-depth interviews on radio station WBUR. Despite the constricting effect of merger mania, many newspapers continue to provide a healthy stream of reporting and reflection. I have benefited greatly from articles in the *Atlanta Journal-Constitution, Boston Globe, Christian Science Monitor, Houston Chronicle, Los Angeles Times, Miami Herald, St. Louis Post-Dispatch, Seattle Times, Wall Street Journal,* and *Washington Post,* where several of my first critiques of the Bush administration appeared, and from essays in *Atlantic Monthly, The Nation, The New York Review of Books, The New York Times Magazine, The New Yorker,* and *Vanity Fair.* A reality check from Europe has been provided by the British Broadcasting Company, *The Economist, The Guardian, The Observer, Financial Times,* and by several French, German, and East European sources. Tapping the resources of the Internet and e-mail, Dr. Carole Wolman supplied me with a wide range of reportage and opinion about U.S. politics.

Professors David Mayers and David Scott Palmer at Boston University, and Leon F. Litwack, University of California, Berkeley, helped me assess the Bush administration's role in history. Dr. Audrey Amrein-Beardsley and Professor David C. Berliner of Arizona State University reviewed the chapter on education.

Boston University students Courtney Stockland and Dino Laverghetta did background research and helped organize the book's many components. Ali Ho Clemens helped to unravel problems in the human-machine interface. Business consultant Ralph Levy reviewed the entire manuscript and made valuable suggestions regarding style and content. My neighbor Larry Osterweil helped to sort cartoons and sustain any flagging spirits. Several denizens of the North Suburban YMCA locker room in Woburn, Massachusetts, also spurred this book—either by their devotion or their animosity to its protagonists.

Believing in and dedicated to this project, publisher Robert S. Brown edited the manuscript and provided essential moral and material support. James Pepe supervised production at Outland Books while Outland's Graphic Design Coordinator, Denice Stowe created the stunning front cover. Thanks also to Carole Juarez at The Lynnx Group for her innovative and wide-ranging PR support. Further thanks goes to Donna Himelfarb for essential editorial assistance and proof reading.

A new U.S. citizen, Anna Sophia Clemens, arrived in the United States from China as this book went to press. May it help to make her life, her native and new homelands, and all the world safer and more salubrious.

W. Clemens

Fewer and fewer newspapers today have the courage to print controversial cartoons and commentary, afraid of offending readers who disagree with their content. I've been lucky this past 25 years to work for one of these courageous papers. My thanks to *The Miami Herald*, publisher Alberto Ibarguen and my editor, Joe Oglesby, for originally publishing these works.

This business is a demanding one with relentless daily deadlines that must be met, a task made less difficult by a supportive family. Thank you, Danielle, Elizabeth and Spencer.

J. Morin

"I think we agree, the past is over."

George W. Bush
May 10, 2000

Introduction

HOW COULD SO MUCH GO SO WRONG SO QUICKLY?

Bushed! Drained. Wasted. Its military muscles spit-polished but its moral authority and treasury dramatically diminished. That's the United States after one term of George W. Bush's presidency. America and the world have been ambushed by a bush-league top gun and his passionate conservative aides-de-camp who wage guerrilla operations, often from "undisclosed locations".

How could the world's only superpower be so rich, so powerful and so influential in 2000 only to descend into a swirl of financial and moral bankruptcy just a year or two later? How could a country that effectively served as a bulwark of international peace and security in the 1990s become a rogue outlaw virtually overnight?

The steep decline began with a stolen election. It continued with a presidency that, even though it lacked a popular mandate, acted to promote the narrow interests of a few. Passionate conservatives who bankrolled the election campaign kept their families rolling in stock dividends, bond coupons and numbered off-shore accounts. They called themselves "compassionate conservatives" but were neither compassionate nor conservative. They were passionate about looting the public weal for private gain, aided by government action and inaction.

Here was larceny on a vast scale: Public goods—clean air, clean water, public lands—would be violated to enrich a few thousand Bush cronies while most of the population suffered. A huge surplus in the U.S. Treasury would soon be transformed into a growing mountain of public debt—abetted by waves of tax cuts, mainly for the wealthy, and by military expenditures that enriched the military-industrial complex.

Though 9/11 indeed demonstrated a serious global threat from al Qaeda, the Bush team used this threat to justify a host of measures to advance its kleptocrat agenda, justifying virtually anything—even drilling for oil in Alaska—as part of the war on terrorism.

How and why did the U.S. fall so far so fast? Here we will cut through the thicket and expose the role of one constant in the whole picture: The rulers' lust for power and wealth. Speaking pieties about faith and freedom, the Bush team has labored to maximize its own power and wealth and that of its patrons. A Marxist would say that some of the country's richest capitalists put their man in office and got him to serve their class interests. While acting as Marx predicted, Dubya and his entourage seemed to implement the advice that Machiavelli provided to the princes of Renaissance Italy.

Be a lion and a fox, Machiavelli urged the aspiring princes. Be strong and wily. The criterion of success is that you obtain, hold and expand your power. If you do this, people will forget if you neglect "law" or "principle". Machiavelli emphasized executive action—*esecuzione*. The prince must be a powerful executive—unfettered by courts or legislatures. He must act forcefully to execute commands, policies—whatever must be done. Indeed, the first rule is to stage executions: Capital punishment. Law and justice are not the point. Executions are needed to intimidate others and remind all who is boss.

A second guideline: Use war and foreign policy to enhance power at home as well as abroad. Foreign crises justify emergency rule and even more power to the executive.

Third: Act as though you execute the will of some third party—best of all, God.

Fourth: Understand that the only important difference between governments is that some succeed and others fail in gaining and holding power—not whether the people or a prince seems to rule.

Fifth: To underscore that you are strong and decisive, you must sometimes act with suddenness. Surprise others and keep them off guard.

Sixth: Envelop your plans and actions in secrecy.

Finally: Recognize the need for one alone—*uno solo*—to make decisions and execute them.

The bottom line for the Bush White House as well as Machiavelli: Might makes right.

These views are not just short-sighted but obsolete. Case histories in every realm show that treating others as if we inhabit a zero-sum world, where only one side can win, sometimes produces short-term profits, but tends to backfire over time. One of the great advances in social science since Plato, Machiavelli and Marx is the insight that human relationships often blend opposing interests, and that skillful players can generate mutual gain.[1] To do so, however, requires mutual respect, openness and dialogue—not brutal and sudden exercises of force. Another advance is the insight that individuals and groups survive and prosper, not by rugged individualism, but by self-organized cooperation from the bottom up.[2]

Rule by *uno solo* in modern times has not worked. The top-down rule of Soviet and Chinese Communists yielded not just economic disaster but also democide, politicide and genocide. Hitler followed Machiavelli's maxims. Nazi Germany absorbed Austria and Czechoslovakia without a fight. Soon Hitler plunged Germany into a two-front war that quickly destroyed the Third Reich. Machiavellians started most of the 20th century's major wars and then lost them.

The greatest achievements of the United States at home and abroad have arisen from policies quite the opposite from those advocated by Machiavelli and practiced—if not preached—by George W. Bush. In the 20th century Americans made great progress in creating a society of equal opportunity and mutual respect. Incomes gradually increased while a growing web of institutions aided the needy. When Theodore Roosevelt busted trusts, this was not for show but for real. When Henry Ford paid workers a decent wage, this was also for real. They could buy the cars they made. When women got the vote, they used it. When Franklin Roosevelt gave "fireside chats" by radio, he did not bully or intimidate but persuaded and co-opted. He, and most presidents after him, seldom commanded action. They consulted with experts, explained their thoughts to the people, and then worked with Congress to get the appropriate legislation.

When Lyndon Johnson and Richard Nixon pursued the Indochina wars with sudden moves, orchestrated in secret, and without sharing all the facts with the public, disaster struck. In nearly all cases where the U.S. attempted "Machiavellian" dirty tricks to overthrow other governments, the long-term consequences proved horrendous: Iran 1953, Guatemala 1954, Vietnam 1963, Chile 1973. The jury is still out on the consequences of the Iraq War, but the deceptions that fueled it already haunt the Bush administration.

America's greatest achievements abroad—the Marshall Plan and NATO—show that Machiavellian tactics are not necessary to do well in world affairs. The reconstruction of Europe and formation of a prosperous and secure trans-Atlantic community arose from a quest for mutual benefit, planned and conducted in the open.[3] This strategy aimed at mutual gain but demanded that each actor contribute what it could. It guarded against Machiavellians, who were ready to exploit others' generosity for one-sided profit.

To get ahead in the world, brute strength and cunning do not suffice. Neither does unlimited faith in human goodness. The best working proposition is that all humans have become interdependent—mutually vulnerable to each other. We are linked so closely that we can readily hurt—or help—one another. Since our relationships are a blend of opposing and shared interests, we need dialogue on how to promote mutual gain. A mutual gain orientation based on conditional cooperation is the key to enhancing the long-term interests of all Americans and all humanity. Indeed, concerted action for mutual gain is probably necessary to save the biosphere—the thin membrane of soil, water and air on which all life depends.[4]

A mutual gain orientation advanced U.S. policies at home and abroad in the 1990s. It was challenged by Newt Gingrich and some other Republican radicals in Congress, but Gingrich was expelled and the others held in check. The orientation helped put America on top of the world at the outset of a new millennium.

As we see in this book, however, a cabal of greedy manipulators seized power and took over Washington in 2001. In previous times, many of America's greatest presidents had personal fortunes before they entered politics—among them George Washington, Theodore and Franklin Roosevelt, John F. Kennedy. But these men did not exploit the presidency for private or family gain. On the contrary, they felt a sort of *noblesse oblige*.[5] The Bush dynasty and its supporters were already quite wealthy in 2000-2001, but they wanted more. The Bushes interlocked government, business and social ties to grow family wealth and power.[6] The family and its co-conspirators raised hypocrisy to new levels, often masking their designs with claims to a nearly divine mission.

The United States under the Bush team spends ever more on defense but is less secure. Corporate bosses receive large bonuses but most Americans are poorer than they were in 2000. Most Americans face higher medical bills with less help from the government or private insurance. Pollution, as well as global warming, increases. Teachers give more tests but kids are not better educated. Some families get vouchers for private schools while public schools are shortchanged. The White House becomes ever more secretive. Except for the right to carry firearms, the Bill of Rights shrinks. Doubts about American democracy mount—at home as well as abroad. Uncle Sam is widely seen as a petulant bully on the world stage—one that speaks loudly and also wields a big stick. He is no longer viewed as an honest broker, good at mediating others' quarrels.

A true conservative in the Teddy Roosevelt mold would seek to maintain and enhance the common good—within the United States and, when possible, worldwide. A compassionate conservative would provide a serious program to help the less fortunate get on their feet. But George W. Bush and his backers have been more passionate than compassionate—passionate about enriching their already bulging bank accounts. Indeed, they give conservatism a bad name, for they pillage more than they preserve.

A wise conservative would surely try to maintain America's status as the world's leading power—one that gets its way mainly by persuasion and example, not by threats or unilateral actions that goad others to resist and undermine America's lead. But Bush and his advisers often seem intent on thumbing their noses at the world. Unlike America's Founding Fathers, the Bush team does not show a "decent respect to the opinions of mankind". Reversing the wisdom of Dale Carnegie, they lose friends and inspire foes.

A former flower child recalled the 1960s: Then, "we thought America was being run by the corporate military-industrial white male power structure. We were certain there was a right-wing conspiracy. We thought civil liberties and free speech were imperiled.... We had reason to believe there was corporate malfeasance and Wall Street was bad. We worried that the government was backing coups in Latin America. We assumed that powerful people were rigging elections. We feared there were people who wanted to blast roads through forests and rip up the tundra." Now, some forty years later, this veteran of the 1960s concluded, "all our worst paranoid nightmares are coming true." How did this happen?

Passionate conservatives waged a very determined, well-organized, and well-financed campaign to regain power and carry out an ultra right-wing revolution. Their greed and ambition also got help from a silent and often selfish majority. Many former activists from the Age of Aquarius gave up and collapsed into an Age of Acquiescence.[7]

"You can fool some of the people some of the time." Mr. Bush's smirk, promises, and his deceptions suggest a confidence that voters can be manipulated to believe almost anything. Fearing another 9/11, many Americans continue to assume that George W. and his key collaborators are doing what's best for the country. If they review the story told in these pages, they may reach the opposite conclusion. The analysis tries to "connect the dots" to suggest what they all mean. This book—its sometimes acrid humor reinforced by hard facts and analysis—strips away the gloss from the dark aims and destructive policies of the Bush White House. New facts and interpretations will surely emerge, but this book tells the story of what probably ranks as the worst administration in U.S. history.

Walter C. Clemens, Jr.

Chapter 1

BAD FOR TEXAS, WORSE FOR AMERICA:
PRIVILEGE WITHOUT HEART OR PRINCIPLE

George W. Bush absorbed Machiavelli's teaching that the only principle in politics is to achieve, hold and expand power. Dubya acted very much like a Machiavellian executive as he wheeled and dealed in business, governed Texas and loose cannoned from the White House. He followed in the footsteps of forebearers who, starting in World War I, helped to run and finance America's military-industrial complex. Dubya's grandfather, Prescott Bush (later a Senator from Connecticut), helped arrange supplies for Hitler's war machine—such as tetraethyl lead for the Luftwaffe—as late as 1938. Prescott and other progenitors were also associated with World War II and Cold War intelligence—connections that overlapped with their business interests in Cuba and the Dominican Republic, as well as in Europe. Some analysts think it likely that Dubya's father had been recruited by the CIA at Yale. The future 41st president performed valiantly in World War II, but he certainly exaggerated the extent to which he ventured west and struck oil on his own.[1] He managed to link the Bush dynasty to Enron and the House of Saud.[2]

Born on July 6, 1946, George W. went east and attended some of the world's best schools—Andover, Yale, and the Harvard Business School. Somewhere along the way, he absorbed Machiavelli's basic advice: Use whatever means will help you succeed.

Young George did not apply himself in school, but privilege and connections can compensate for some deficiencies. Starting in 1975, Dubya raked in, lost and made lots of money—first in energy and then in baseball. Though defeated in a race for Congress in 1976, George W. later won the governor's office in Texas—in 1994 and again in 1998.

Determined to prevent Al Gore from succeeding Bill Clinton in the White House, top Republicans and their financial backers chose George W. as the man they would run for president in 2000. Was Dubya running on his father's coattails? Of course not, he replied. Did he have a drinking problem? No—that was a youthful excess he renounced at age 40.

Whatever else, George W. had a golden touch. Dubya's number one career patron, the Enron Corporation, delivered some $550,025 to his two gubernatorial runs and 2000 presidential campaign. Other major donors are listed later in "Bushonomics". In 2000 Dubya spent some $89 million just to nail down the Republican presidential nomination. His bulging coffers enabled him to spurn $15 million in federal matching funds and before the Republican convention he spent more than twice the ceiling allowed for candidates accepting federal money. Altogether the Bush campaign collected $191 million—far more than Gore's $133 million total.[3]

When Florida's electoral votes were disputed after the November 2000 election, Bush collected an extra $14 million to fly in staff, hire lawyers and bus partisans around the state; Gore raised less than $4 million to challenge hanging chads and other irregularities.

CLASS CREDENTIALS

The "education president" who would promote testing as the way to save America's youth had been an indifferent pupil at Andover, Yale and the Harvard Business School. Still, he passed one vital test—in his school years and later: He scored A+ on family wealth and influence. What about his C record at Yale? Boosters said this showed him to be a man of the people, a regular guy—not an elitist. If George was still just a grown-up frat boy, one Texas magazine opined, this was all for the good. After all, the French Revolution extolled liberty, equality and fraternity! The magazine ignored evidence that Dubya showed little devotion to equality. Hispanics complained that George W. had never in all his years as governor looked in on the 400,000 plus people living in shabby *colonias* near the U.S.-Mexican border—in contrast to Al Gore, who had visited them at least twice before the 2000 election campaign even began.

SUPER PATRIOT UNTESTED

George W.'s flying potential was so evident during the Vietnam War that, despite getting the lowest possible passing score, he was leapfrogged over 150 applicants and awarded one of two remaining slots in the Texas Air National Guard. Asked about his motives, Bush stated in 1990 that he was unwilling to mutilate himself to get a deferment or go to Canada and therefore chose to learn how to fly. Asked by the Guard if he would volunteer for overseas duty, he checked the box "do not volunteer". He pledged to serve six years in the Guard and to make flying a lifetime pursuit, but he often did not show up for training in Texas. After four years he left for Alabama, where he was suspended from service for failing to take a physical.[4]

THE TERMINATOR

George W. laid claim to being a law-and-order governor—tough on drugs and on all crime. Consciously or not, Dubya followed Machiavelli's advice and allowed Texas to execute more people annually than all other states combined. In 2000 the state broke the national record (set in Texas a few years before) for executions in a single year. That year there were 85 executions in the United States—40 of them in Texas, followed by Oklahoma (11) and Virginia (8). In 2000 some 450 Texans awaited execution, the highest per capita rate in the country. California, with one-third more residents, had a higher total on death row, 586, but executed just one person that year. Trying to justify the high rate of executions, some Texans noted that they had more murders than elsewhere and therefore needed more capital punishment.

In his six years as governor, George W. presided over more executions than any governor in U.S. history—152 (names of those executed at: www.wf.net/~connally/apdxAbush.html). Was this record a cause for pride and pleasure or for shame and pain? Was it a reason to vote for George W. as a firm enforcer or to despise and reject him as one indifferent to life and justice? How much "compassion" had he shown? Governor Bush sponsored

tax cuts in Texas that depleted an already very weak support system for the mentally retarded, some of whom landed on death row.

Despite requests for clemency from religious leaders ranging from the pope to Pat Robertson, Governor Bush denied all appeals from a defendant in a case where there was no physical evidence and only one eyewitness—one who twice failed to identify the suspect until prompted by the police—plus two witnesses who placed the suspect elsewhere.

The governor claimed that he and the system did not err. "I analyze each case when it comes across my desk. And as far as I'm concerned, there has not been one innocent person executed since I've been the governor" (*Washington Post*, June 22, 2000). But the quality of legal representation for indigent defendants was often low. A majority of those executed in Texas during the Bush years were represented by lawyers who had been warned or even punished by the state bar association. Indeed, after George W. left Austin for Washington, Texas lifted the death sentence from one defendant convicted on Dubya's watch because the man's court-appointed lawyer had fallen asleep during the trial.

Capital punishment in Texas, as in most states, had racist overtones because many of the condemned were not just indigent but also—disproportionately—black. Of the 85 persons executed nationwide in 2000, 35 were black and 49 white. Later we examine the cocaine sting against "niggers" endorsed by the Texas Narcotics Control Board while Mr. Bush was governor.

FINALITY, PUSHED BY JIM CROW IN CYBERSPACE

Gore won more popular votes than Bush in the election held on November 7, 2000. But which candidate won a majority in the electoral college? The answer hinged on Florida, where Dubya's brother, Jeb, was governor. On November 20 the Florida Secretary of State, Katherine Harris, ruled that George W. had won the state by 537 votes. But Democrats complained about many irregularities such as the very confusing "butterfly ballot" used in largely Democratic Palm Beach County, where the votes of some 30,000 persons were disqualified because they had "overvoted" or "undervoted". In other Florida precincts voters were turned away because their names did not appear on a master list that had not been updated. Blacks and Latinos complained they had been intimidated by police. One in every twenty-seven ballots was discarded for irregularities in precincts that Gore won, compared to just one in forty where Bush won.

As many as 50,000 individuals, most of them likely to vote for Gore, were wrongfully denied access to the polls in November 2000, because their names had been purged from Florida's list of eligible voters in procedures that Greg Palast calls "Jim Crow in Cyberspace". The purge list was prepared by a private firm that later admitted making many errors, but explained that the list was supposed to be vetted by Florida authorities, who happened to be Republican.[4] In the middle of this fracas, the Republican candidate raised doubts about whether he could pass an elementary civics test. Dubya declared that "the legislature's job is to write law. It's the executive branch's

job to interpret law" (*The New York Times*, November 23, 2000). George W. was coming close to Machiavelli's view that the executive should control both the courts and the legislature.[5]

Bush's Republican team called for finality; Democrats for fairness. Florida's secretary of state was hardly a model of impartiality, for Ms. Harris had co-chaired the Bush campaign in the state! She pressed the Florida Supreme Court to halt manual recounts that had begun in several counties. But on November 21 the high court ordered hand counts to continue, giving counties five days to complete them. When this deadline expired, Ms. Harris certified that Bush had won Florida's entire electoral vote. She turned away the results from Palm Beach County, which arrived two hours late. When Gore asked for a recount of some 14,000 undervotes, however, the Florida high court agreed. As Bush's lead slipped to 193 votes, his legal team asked the U.S. Supreme Court to intervene and halt the hand counting.

Worried that a large-scale vote recount might take place in Florida, the state's Republican-dominated legislature prepared in early December, 2000, to convene a special session to appoint the state's 25 presidential electors. On December 4 top Republicans said that only a quick concession by candidate Gore or a decisive ruling by the Florida Supreme Court against a recount could derail a special session. The state's Republican leaders were spared the political risks of calling a special session when the U.S. Supreme Court ruled that the Democrats' jig was up.[6]

THE SUPREME COURT DECIDES THE PEOPLE'S CHOICE

On December 9 the Supreme Court issued a stay to stop the recount. On December 12 the judges ruled 5-4 that there should be no further counting of votes in Florida except for absentee ballots. In an unsigned decision the court majority reversed the Florida high court order for a recount. "It is obvious," five judges agreed, "that the recount cannot be conducted in compliance with the requirements of equal protection and due process without substantial additional work." The argument that the constitutional guarantee of equal protection would apply to vote counting in Florida was so far-fetched that employing it was initially dismissed by Dubya's legal team, yet finally adopted by five Supreme Court judges. Giving Florida's electoral vote to Bush, the court decided the national election—271 electoral votes for Bush, and 266 for Gore.

Dissenting Judge John Paul Stevens said the Supreme Court should never have intervened. "Although we may never know with certainty the identity of the winner of this year's presidential election, the identity of the loser is perfectly clear. It is the nation's confidence in the judge as an impartial guardian of the rule of law." Justice Steven Breyer added: "By embroiling ourselves in this political maelstrom," the Supreme Court risked "a self-inflicted wound...that may harm not just the court, but the nation."

Had democracy in the United States ever suffered such a blow as that delivered by the highest court in the land? Some Americans were shocked to learn that their government had a role in *coups d'état* in Iran, Guatemala, Vietnam, and elsewhere. Many members of Congress were furious to learn that the Reagan Administration had deceived even them about Iran-Contra. But no anti-democratic action taken by any authority in Washington in the 20th century approached the Supreme Court's decision to cut off inquiries into the will of Florida voters and thus permit a candidate lacking a popular majority to become president.

After aborting self-rule in the United States, how could official Washington purport to foster democracy abroad? By what right could the U.S. government send election observers anywhere—even to Haiti or Azerbaijan? Former President Jimmy Carter said that his election monitors would never work in a country with so many structural election irregularities as the state of Florida. Within two years, however, the man whose agents stole the Florida election presided over "regime changes" in Afghanistan and Iraq, the latter depicted as a strategy to democratize the Middle East.

SHEIKS AND MOONIES HELP THE
DYNASTY AND VICE VERSA

As the 43rd president settled into the White House, the 41st often received what CIA agents called the "President's Daddy's daily briefing". Poppy at times took the initiative to advise his son on foreign affairs. Thus, the former prez sent Dubya a memo in June 2001, advising him to re-engage with Communist North Korea. In the first half of 2001 the ex-prez twice phoned Crown Prince Abdulla of Saudi Arabia to assure him that George W.'s heart was in the right place—even though Dubya seemed to favor Israeli Prime Minister Ariel Sharon against the Palestinians. But whatever Washington did was in the right place—even though Dubya seemed to favor Israeli Prime to placate Saudi Arabia achieved only limited success. Riyadh refused to extradite eleven suspects in the 1996 Al Khobar truck bombing that killed nineteen U.S. servicemen and, in 2001, placed new restrictions on the ordnance Americans could bring into Saudi Arabia. Many Saudis took umbrage when Americans blamed the desert kingdom for furnishing most of the 9/11 killers.

While George W. was a son of Midland, Texas, the father was a man of the world. So devoted was the elder George to global understanding that he flew to Buenos Aires in 1996 to endorse Sun Muyung Moon's efforts to found *Tiempos de Mundo*, a Latin American equivalent to the *Washington Times*, a paper the former president told Argentines had brought "sanity" to the U.S. capital (Reuters, November 25, 1996). Perhaps Bush knew nothing about the Moonie agenda for world domination, their use of brainwashing or the long jail term served by the cult's founder for evading U.S. taxes. After all, the former head of the CIA could not be expected to know much about a cleric who would send a private plane to Texas so George the Elder and Barbara could fly in comfort to Argentina, where they stayed in the home of President Carlos Menem. The Argentine leader later told reporters that Bush claimed to be only a mercenary who did not really know Moon. "Bush told me he came and charged money to do it" (*La Nacion*, November 26,1996). The Bush dynasty seemed to respond to bribes more than the many professors, who turned down fees of several thousand dollars and foreign junkets to add luster to Unification Church projects. In September 1995, George and Barbara gave six speeches in Asia for the Women's Federation for World Peace, a group led by Moon's wife (*The Washington Post*, September 15, 1995). The Moonies paid the Bush family from one to ten million dollars in the 1990s.

JUST SAY NO

Early to bed, early to rise, makes a man healthy and wealthy. George W. would enjoy being president, predicted David G. Winter, a professor of political psychology. However, Winter's study of "motive profile" also suggested that the younger Bush would be "a more aggressive and less entrepreneurial version of his father." Dubya's inauguration speech used the word "not" almost 17 times per 1,000 words—more than any previous president. This, said Winter, showed "activity inhibition"—typically high in people who give up alcohol or do not drink.[7] Less kind and gentle than his father, George II looked more like a Machiavellian prince than the old king, the 41st president.

"The reason I believe in a large tax cut because it's what I believe."

George W. Bush
December 18, 2000

Chapter 2

BUSHONOMICS: VOODOO ECONOMICS OR KLEPTOMANIA?

Back in 1980, George Bush the Elder lambasted Ronald Reagan's "supply side" tax cuts as "voodoo economics." But voters twice made Reagan president with George H. W. Bush serving faithfully as his vice president. Many years later, when George the Elder became president and welshed on his "no new taxes" pledge, many conservatives cried out, "Betrayal!" George the Younger did not make his father's mistake. As governor he kept the Lone Star State free of all taxes except sales taxes and license fees—resulting in too little revenue to meet basic needs.[1]

Bushonomics is Reaganomics beyond the pale. It is kleptocracy—a greedy and corrupt regime that robs the public. Kleptomaniacs feel an obsessive drive to rob even without material need. The leading Bush kleptocrats have been multimillionaires for years, but they continue to exploit public positions for private gain.[2]

Bushonomics generated a zero-sum conflict between Americans. Seldom in U.S. history had so few benefited at the expense of the many. The Bush system violated intergenerational equity—the principle that each generation should pass on a better world to its progeny. Today's children and theirs will have to shoulder and pay off the public debts rung up by George W. Bush's kleptocracy.

Bushonomics is straightforward: Cut taxes, but mainly for the rich. Give preferential treatment to the petroleum and other resource-extracting industries; privatize retirement funds; starve "the beast"—what passionate conservatives call the welfare state. Meanwhile, preach self-reliance and promise that tax breaks will stimulate investment and generate jobs—just as Reagan claimed for his "trickle down" approach. If seniors insist on prescription drug benefits, structure the program to ensure a bonanza for drug makers.

Bushonomics showed that Karl Marx had great insight into the ways that economics shape politics. As evident in Table 2.1, corporate America backed George Bush and his business-friendly economics in the 2000 elections.

Defense companies donated over four times more to Bush than to Gore.

SOURCE: Center for Responsive Politics

Industry sector	For Bush	For Gore
Finance, insurance, real estate	$16	$5
Miscellaneous businesses	$8	$3
Lawyers and lobbyists	$7	$6
Health	$4	$1
Construction	$4	$1
Communications and electronics	$3.3	$2.5
Energy and natural resources	$2.8	$0.3
Agribusiness	$2.6	$0.3
Ideology/Single issue	$2.5	$0.9
Transportation	$2.3	$0.3
Defense	$181 k	$40 k
Labor	$40 k	$100 k

Table 2.1 Contributions by Sector to the 2000 Presidential Elections
(in millions except for Defense and Labor, in thousands)

Each of 214 members of the Pioneer Club raised more than $100,000 for Bush. Among them: AG Spanos (finance and real estate, Stockton, Ca.), $877,000; Sam Fox (CEO of Harbour Group in St. Louis and a key figure in a national Republican Jewish coalition), $831,000; Kenneth Lay (CEO of Enron), $574,550; Louis A. Beecherl, Jr., (owner of Beecherl Investments in Dallas, energy and natural resources), $446,350; and Herbert F. Collins (chair of Boston Capital Partners and leader of the elder Bush's New England campaign in 1992), $303,719. One hand washed the other. President George W. Bush did not neglect the material interests of those who helped him.

SLEIGHT OF HAND

Dubya told Americans they could have it all—lower taxes, beefed-up defense, better education, bigger agricultural subsidies, plus a prescription drug benefit. To make this voodoo economics plausible required much sleight-of-hand accounting. Bush signed his first tax package into law on June 7, 2001. It provided for $1.35 trillion in tax cuts over the next nine years, to be financed by a recently acquired budget surplus which was already vanishing. Despite huge security outlays after 9/11/01 and a sagging economy, the White House rammed through two more tax cut programs in 2002 and 2003.

A MAGIC ELIXIR

Guided by divine inspiration and/or the material interests of his backers, George W. unveiled a panacea for whatever ailed the country, namely tax

cuts. When times were bad, tax relief would put money into the pockets of consumers and the investment tills of manufacturers. When times were good, tax reductions would reward people who had paid high taxes in rough times. Meanwhile, if gasoline prices inched up, tax relief would ease the pain. The U.S. Treasury could help you to help Exxon. Was this not a win-win outcome?

DIVINE INTERVENTION?

Just before the November 2000, election, George W. said of Democrats: "They want the federal government controlling Social Security like it's some kind of federal program." As candidate and then as president, George W. saw Social Security as a private affair.

In 2001 Dubya said that the Social Security system could be repaired painlessly by allowing younger workers to divert a portion of their payroll tax into individual accounts. However, he failed to explain how the U.S. Treasury could send checks each month to retirees if younger people still working did not regularly replenish its coffers. Nor did he explain how those invested in stocks could base their retirement income on assets whose value cycled up and down in huge waves. Multimillionaires, however, could sleep better knowing their heirs would be spared "death" (estate) taxes.

DEEP POCKETS—YOUR SOCIAL SECURITY!

The true cost of the tax cut shenanigans appeared immediately. The U.S. Treasury had hoped to pay down $57 billion in marketable debt in the third quarter of 2001. Instead, it had to raise government debt. Also, the Congressional Budget Office reported in late August 2001, that the federal government would have to tap the Social Security "trust fund" for $9 billion to pay current bills.[3]

The 2001 tax cut, if fully phased in, would deliver 42% of its benefits to the richest 1% of Americans. The 2003 cut gave most of its largesse to those with incomes over $1 million per year—a mere 0.13% of the population. How could the White House sell such policies to the public? It shamelessly fudged the numbers. The administration said that 92 million Americans would receive an average tax cut of $1,083. But this "average" factored in the 50 million taxpayers who received nothing and the very wealthiest who received huge tax windfalls. In fact, about half of American families received less than $100.

CONTRIBUTIONS AND/OR VOTES WELCOME

The White House conned the public with some $38 billion in tax rebate checks mailed out in summer 2001. Each taxpayer (about 92 million) got $300 (minus any funds still owed the government). These munificent rebates were a political down payment on a $1.35 trillion tax cut due to unfold in the years ahead, mostly for people in the highest tax brackets.

Before the money arrived in the mail, the Internal Revenue Service sent a letter to each taxpayer saying that relief was on the way. It read like a telegram to a sweepstakes winner. Each taxpayer learned that new legislation just signed by President George W. Bush provided "immediate tax relief in 2001 and long-term tax relief for years to come." Left unsaid was an additional line that might have read: "Please show your gratitude by voting

for this most generous president and his friends the next time around." Each
mailing—the promissory notes and the actual checks—cost more than $20
million. However, 30 million Americans—so poor they paid no taxes—received no such messages from the IRS.

SAFE HAVENS

Characterizing the Internal Revenue Service as storm troopers breaking
down the doors of God-fearing, law-abiding citizens, Congress demanded a
kinder and gentler IRS—especially as it dealt with rich folks. After Congress
cut the agency's budget and staff in the 1990s, IRS computers focused on
arithmetical errors in low—and medium—income returns. IRS auditors
reviewed very few returns on the high end. Dubya's first treasury secretary,
Paul O'Neill, led a charge in 2001 to sabotage international cooperation to
crack down on tax havens in the Cayman Islands and elsewhere. American firms needed to shelter their foreign earnings to be competitive, he explained. The tourist literature for another tax haven, the Turks and Caicos
Islands, reported in 2003 that, despite tighter regulations, the number of tax
lawyers and accountancies there had jumped from a handful in the 1980s to
the thousands.

After reviewing the assorted tax breaks (valued at $65 billion a year)
the U.S. grants to exporters, including giants such as Microsoft and Boeing,

the World Trade Organization ruled in August 2003 that these subsides are illegal because they put foreign rivals at a competitive disadvantage. Accordingly, the European Union Commission announced in February 2004 that it would impose some $4 billion in trade sanctions unless Congress promptly eliminated overseas tax breaks. The taxes Boeing did not pay, of course, were shouldered by other tax payers.

DON'T THE RICH DESERVE A BREAK?

Kleptocracy requires some secrecy at the top and some naiveté and wishful thinking at the middle and lower ranks of society. By July 2002, however, two-thirds of Americans had concluded that big business exerted too much influence on the Bush administration. A New York Times/CBS Poll published on July 18 found that 62% of respondents believed that corporate accounting scandals were a serious problem for the U.S. economy. One-half thought that the president's proposals for reforming corporate accounting aimed to protect large corporations rather than ordinary Americans. Nearly half thought Bush and Vice President Cheney were hiding something about their past business practices—over 9% accused both men of lying. Half the respondents doubted that Mr. Bush was running the government.

Despite everything, Bush's popularity rating was still high in 2002—70% in July (down from 89% just after 9/11). Some 52% approved of how he dealt with the economy. And 68% believed that Bush cared about ordinary people. Some 43% said Bush had behaved ethically in his past business practices, more than double the 21% who doubted him.[4]

STEEL TILL IT HURTS

When Bush raised tariffs on steel imports in 2002, European and other steel producers cried foul. In 2003, the World Trade Organization ruled that these import duties violated WTO rules and that other nations were entitled to retaliate. Bush then weighed the support he got from steel producing states against the displeasure of auto manufacturers and others who wanted cheap steel. Accordingly, the White House announced in December 2003, that the tariffs had done their job and would be dropped (long before the steel manufacturers had been promised).

The U.S. was suffering de-industrialization. As of December 2003, the U.S. had lost manufacturing jobs for 40 straight months. And Americans depended increasingly on imports. Another reason for job loss, however, was computerized automation: U.S. manufacturers were producing more goods with less labor. To ease the pain of jobs lost in manufacturing, the White House chief economist, a former Harvard professor, tried to count jobs gained in hamburger-flipping as "manufacture".

WHY AMERICA NEEDS CHINA

The percentage of workers filing for unemployment fell below 6% in late 2003, but more than 2 million Americans had been jobless for more than 6 months. Payrolls were 2.4 million less than in early 2001. Dubya conceded on September 5, 2003, that "this economy needs to crank up faster...for somebody to find a job." But he blamed China for keeping its currency cheap so it could sell far more than it buys from America. He did not mention that purchases of U.S. Treasury bonds by China's central bank helped keep U.S. interest rates low. What if China shifted to euros?

WAL-MARTIZATION

As Karl Marx asserted in the Communist Manifesto (1848), capitalism made the world interdependent. Wal-Mart, the largest corporation in the world ($220 billion in revenues) and headed by the richest man in the world, lived by the principles Marx attributed to capitalism: Pay workers a subsistence wage (if that) and don't let them unionize. Buy and sell without regard to national borders. Wal-Mart used to claim, "We Buy American," but in the early 21st century it just waved the flag. The average Wal-Mart worker, according to Jim Hightower, was paid $15,000 a year, while just over one-third received health insurance. On December 17, 2001, the *Wall Street Journal* reported that Wal-Mart was ordered to pay nearly $7 million in fines for disability-screening of job applicants.

Informed in September 2003, that nearly 3 million jobs had disappeared on his watch, Dubya said that the best way to create jobs would be to make the tax cuts permanent. He repeated the shibboleth, "tax cuts mean new jobs for Americans." If unemployment remained close to 6% in 2004, said Senator Joe Lieberman, the only job left to cut by November 2004, would be that of George W. Bush.

SO HOW MUCH DO TAX CUTS COST?

Many Democrats went to bed with the president in the "tax cut hotel." Who could resist the sweet logic of getting everything you want from government while paying lower taxes?

Combined U.S. taxes—local, state and federal—reached nearly 30% of gross domestic product in 2000. Sweden, however, collected 52% of GDP in taxes; France, 46%; and Canada, 38%. After U.S. stock values collapsed and the Bush tax cuts began, the U.S. tax rate declined to about 26% in 2002-2003. This 26% was the same rate that middle-class Americans had paid since the 1970s. For Americans in the top income bracket, however, the rate had declined to 35%—half what it had been in the Nixon years. Aiding the wealthy still more, the Bush team reduced corporate, dividend and estate taxes. By the time the Bush tax cuts take their full effect, rich Americans will enjoy the lowest average tax rates since the Hoover administration.[5]

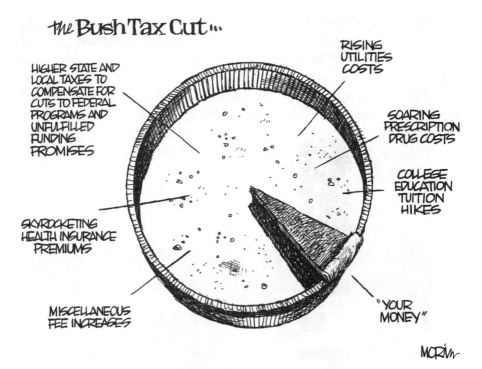

How much of the mounting U.S. budget deficit resulted from tax cuts? According to the Congressional Budget Office, half the $450 billion budget deficit in 2003 (nearly 5% of GDP) is due to Bush tax cuts. Some of the cuts were scheduled to expire some years hence, but this will be hard to accomplish politically. Forecasts show that the budget gap will become a chasm by 2015, if not sooner, as baby boomers retire and claim Social Security and Medicare benefits. The deficit would expand even without the Bush tax cuts. Kept in place, however, they will more than double it. Unless, against the odds, Congress raises taxes, pressure will mount to shrink the welfare programs built up from the New Deal through the Johnson and Nixon years.

In February 2004, the Congressional Budget Office declared that the tax and spending plans in the president's fiscal year 2005 budget would produce a deficit approaching $3 trillion by 2014. Three trillion dollars is nearly one-third of the Gross Domestic Product. (This projection does not include the cost of military operations in Iraq and Afghanistan.)

In February 2004, Federal Reserve Chairman Alan Greenspan and Bush called for cuts in Social Security and Medicare benefits. Greenspan and Bush agreed that the only way to maintain national solvency while retaining tax breaks and huge military outlays was to trim entitlement programs.

According to Greenspan and Bush, government-funded pensions were
the problem even though the Social Security trust fund surplus was expected
to increase in the years ahead (while huge deficits pervaded the rest of the
budget). The most pessimistic projected balance in the Social Security coffers was $5 trillion by the year 2020. Those who wished to "starve the beast"
of big government planned to do so by robbing the pensions of millions of
Americans who had contributed to them throughout their lives—in effect,
forcing the vast majority of retirees to suffer in order to maintain tax breaks
for a wealthy few.

Bushonomics proved to be not only unjust but imprudent. Taking money
from the majority of the elderly to provide a tax break to the wealthiest
Americans would actually *de-stimulate* the economy. Further, making
medical care more expensive for seniors would add to overall medical
costs because it would deter preventive medicine. Much of what President
George W. imposed on the entire country mirrored what Governor Jeb did
to Florida.

RULES—WHO NEEDS THEM?

For much of the 20th century, political reformers enacted regulations that prevented corporate abuse and created assistance programs to protect the needy. Starting in 1980, however, Ronald Reagan and his successors argued that government is the problem—not the solution. They tore away at government regulation of the strong and reduced help for the weak in one sphere after another.

The president, his VP, and much of the cabinet who took power in 2001 had built political careers thundering against regulation while enjoying a cozy camaraderie with firms, such as Enron, that grew fat on deregulation. Many in the Bush entourage had spent years lining their pockets with sweetheart loans, option deals and golden parachutes. In 2000-2001, however, industry giants such as Enron and WorldCom crashed, despite—or due to—false accounting and shady deals assisted by banks and accountancies. Enron employees and unwitting investors were left empty handed after top executives bailed out. Markets were not self-regulating—as we see in Chapter 3.

Chapter 3

SECRETS OF ENERGY: CALIFORNIA DREAMIN'

If some schemer had a magic ring that rendered him invisible, he could do whatever he wished—take whatever goods he pleased, ravish whatever woman he coveted, even kill the king—and he would go undetected. With a twist of the ring, he could become visible again and seem the paragon of virtue. Such an operator was sketched in Plato's *Republic* more than 2000 years ago, but also resembles modern-day operators in real-life Houston, Washington and other power centers.

If someone had such a ring, Glaucon tells Socrates in Plato's tale, he would surely exploit it: No matter what the ring's owner did on the sly, his magic permits him to be known for his virtue. He gets top jobs in government, allies himself by marriage with any family he chooses, becomes a partner in any business, and, having no scruples, turns all these advantages to profit. His religious offerings may even open the door to heaven.

Socrates points out that, over time, feigned honesty will destroy the individual who practices it and throw his entire society off balance. Still, in the short haul, Glaucon's approach can score hefty profits, as when Enron and other energy traders exploited the fuel and electricity demands of California and other states in markets deregulated under President Ronald Reagan and some of his successors.

President George W. Bush and his associates sought to craft several rings like Glaucon's that would permit them to appear as paragons of virtue while they ravished the public. They built one such ring from "executive privilege." George W. used such tools even before he became president. Probably mindful that Richard Nixon had been hoisted on his own petard—the White House tapes—Dubya did all he could to hide or at least blur the record of his exploits, including his close ties to Enron Corporation and its long-time boss, Ken Lay, the lead funder of Dubya's two gubernatorial campaigns and his 2000 run for the White House.

Machiavelli, as we have seen, recommended that the prince act in secret to plan and execute decisive moves. This chapter focuses on the secrecy that enveloped the Bush energy policy. Later we shall see how deception and secrecy were leitmotifs of his actions in many arenas, both domestic and external.

WHAT YOU DON'T KNOW CAN'T HURT ME

In 1997, Governor George W. persuaded the Texas legislature to pass a law allowing governors to store their official papers in a depository other than the state archives. When Mr. Bush became U.S. president, he ordered that his gubernatorial papers be sent 118 miles away to be vaulted in his father's presidential library at Texas A&M University instead of across the street from the Texas Capital in Austin. Why? Did he hope to obstruct access to materials on his contacts with Enron officials? As an official in the Better Government Association of Chicago observed: "Who needs a shredder when you have Daddy's presidential library?"[1]

Like Glaucon, many public figures prefer to keep their mischief from public scrutiny. President George W. sought to expand the practice of executive privilege in unprecedented ways. He went well beyond the schemes pioneered by Nixon and expanded under Ronald Reagan to keep information from Congress, the courts and the public. On November 1, 2001, Dubya issued Executive Order 13233, asserting a hitherto unknown privilege for former presidents to claim executive privilege over their own papers, even if the sitting president disagrees, as well as the right of a sitting president to

privilege a past administration's papers—even if the former president disagrees!

Critics argued that presidential papers are public records—not private possessions. Hence, they should be regulated by statute—not by an executive order. Over time, the papers of a previous president lose any claim to privilege by reason of national security, but Dubya's order set no time limit. Documents relevant to national security are, in any case, protected by other regulations.

Why did Bush stray so far from precedent? The last sentence of the letter announcing his order gave a hint: "This directive again applies also to the vice presidential records of former Vice President George H.W. Bush." Thus, any attempt to link his father to the Iran-Contra scandal could be stalled for the indefinite future. Any less-than-legal actions by the many current holdovers from the previous Reagan and Bush administrations could also be shelved in deep freeze.

In Fall 2001, adding to the movement toward stealth, Attorney General John Ashcroft told federal agencies (including the National Archives administering the Bush presidential library) that they would be vigorously defended when they withheld records requested under the Freedom of Information Act.

THE VP VS. GOVERNMENT INSPECTORS

The General Accounting Office announced in January 2002, that it would take the White House to court—the first time in the 80-year history of the GAO that it would sue the Executive Branch. Why would the nonpartisan investigative arm of Congress take such a radical step? The GAO sought to force the White House to disclose information about meetings held by Vice President Dick Cheney's energy task-force (The National Energy Policy Development Group) with industry executives in 2001 before it recommended an energy strategy focused on construction of new power plants and the opening of environmentally sensitive lands to oil and gas drilling.

Cheney, backed by Bush, refused to comply with the GAO request for energy task force records. The VP said discussions with energy industry officials were necessary to obtain expert advice. The GAO's demands, said President Bush, amounted to "an encroachment on the executive branch's ability to conduct business." The VP told Congress that the GAO lacked authority to seek task-force information and could only review the results of energy programs. On December 9, 2002, the U.S. District Court for the District of Columbia dismissed the GAO suit, ruling that Comptroller General David Walker lacked standing. He did not appeal.

How far the VP was willing to go to mislead Congress and/or buy off the courts became clear in late 2003 and early 2004. On August 25, 2003, the GAO issued its final report on the task force affair. The report revealed that Cheney wrote to Congress on August 2, 2001, claiming that his office had sent the GAO 74 pages of "documents retrieved from the files of the Office of the Vice President responsive to" GAO's inquiry regarding the Energy Task Force's "receipt, disbursement, and use of public funds." But the GAO report stated that the documents were useless. "The materials were virtually impossible to analyze, as they consisted, for example, of pages with dollar amounts but no indication of the nature or purpose of the expenditure." They were "predominantly reimbursement requests, assorted telephone bills and random items, such as the executive director's credit card receipt for pizza." Former White House counsel John Dean inferred that Cheney aimed to deceive Congress, where he served as the chief presiding officer (http://writ. news.findlaw.com/dean/20030829.html). For the text of the August 25, 2003, report, see: http://www.thememoryhole.org/pol/cheney-energy/gao.htm.

Meanwhile, Judicial Watch and the Sierra Club also sued the VP in 2002 to gain access to the energy task force records. When two federal courts approved their request, Cheney appealed to the Supreme Court for relief. In December 2003, the Supreme Court agreed to hear the case. The next month, Cheney sent his plane, Air Force Two, to give Justice Scalia and his daughter a ride so Scalia and the VP could go duck hunting. Though the law demands that a federal judge recuse himself from proceedings where his "impartiality might be questioned", Scalia refused to do so in the Cheney appeal.

Scalia, whom Bush saw as a model for judicial behavior, also failed to recuse himself in a previous case where the dean of the University of Kansas Law School represented the State of Kansas, just two weeks after he had hosted Scalia on a pheasant hunt. Critics said that Scalia's justice was for the birds!

STONEWALLING AROUND THE WHITE HOUSE

Dubya's major financial backer went bottom-up in 2001—the largest bankruptcy in U.S. history. Fortunately for the Bush team, Enron's death throes coincided with heightened concern for homeland security after the terrorist attack of 9/11/01. The vice president and a shadow government retreated to undisclosed locations. The White House suggested that anyone who questioned the administration about anything was unpatriotic. The Afghan campaign and war fever over Iraq in 2002 helped deflect Americans' attention from domestic scandals.

In January 2002, the *San Francisco Chronicle* revealed that Lay had given Cheney a letter detailing the company's arguments against price caps and other regulatory measures intended to curb surging electricity prices in California. A few weeks later, Cheney called price caps "a mistake."

Mr. Cheney assured the public that "there is no evidence to indicate anybody did anything wrong in the administration." But the *Los Angeles Times* derided "Cheney's Stone Wall" and polls taken in January and again in July 2002, showed that more than half the U.S. public thought the Bush team was hiding something or lying about Enron.

THE NEWS: ENRON MAY HAVE MORE
TAX HAVENS THAN HALLIBURTON!

When Enron was formed in 1985, Vice President George Bush pressed Congress to loosen the regulatory straitjacket on public utilities. When the elder Bush became the 41st president, he approved two laws that helped Enron. First, the energy act adopted in 1992 obliged utility companies to transmit electricity shipped by Enron and other marketers. Second, a regulation issued by the Commodity Futures Trading Commission created a legal exemption that permitted Enron to begin trading energy derivatives.

A deregulated Enron rapidly grew from a regional supplier of natural gas to a gargantuan buyer and seller of gas, electricity, broadband on fiber optic cable, data storage and even water. By 2000, it was the 7th largest corporation in the U.S. and 16th in the world. The Bush family and its retainers clustered around Enron "like bees around a honeycomb," wrote Kevin Phillips. In 2001, however, Enron tanked and declared bankruptcy. It had played an elaborate shell game, hiding debts in some 800 offshore tax havens, Enron's top brass had raked in millions but then left most company employees and stockholders empty-handed. Some reports held that Dick Cheney's old employer, Halliburton, had less than 100 off-shore money laundering operations.

Having struck hard at California consumers of gas and electricity, Enron had helped create a crisis in which demands were voiced to recall recently elected Governor Gray Davis. Whatever his faults, the deficit that grew under Davis amounted to less than 1% of the debt burden the Bush team spawned for the entire country.

UNREGULATED GROPING

California suffered electricity shortages and dramatic price rises in 2001. On May 4, shortly before visiting California, President Bush declared: "What people need to hear loud and clear is that we're running out of energy in

America." Therefore, he said, "It is so important for this nation to improve its infrastructure, so we cannot only deliver supplies, but we need to go find new supply.... You cannot conserve your way to energy independence." The policy conclusion was: Don't mess with the markets. Bush spokesman Ari Fleisher said: "The last thing that anybody would want to do is to create price controls," because they would create more shortages.

Enron's Ken Lay also visited California in May. On May 17, 2001, at the Peninsula Hotel in Beverly Hills, he met with Los Angeles Mayor Richard Riordon, convicted junk bond swindler Michael Milliken and potential California governor Arnold Schwarzenegger, renowned for his energy in unregulated groping. The context was itself gripping: California had suffered three sets of rolling blackouts and huge increases in consumer energy prices. But Enron was also under siege. Its stock had lost half its value since January. California's Lt. Governor Cruz Bustamente was gathering evidence that Enron had manipulated the market (by fraudulent reporting of sales, megawatt laundering and fake power delivery scheduling). Later, he filed a suit demanding that Enron repay California some $9 billion (more than sufficient to cover the state's 2003-2004 debt of $8 billion). What passed between Lay and his Peninsula Hotel interlocutors is not yet public. At a minimum Lay probably wanted a continuation of the deregulated conditions that permitted Enron to gouge California consumers.[2]

Dubya's hatchet man, Karl Rove, pulled out all stops in 2003 to back the initiative to recall Governor Davis. On October 14, 2003, after Davis was recalled, the Foundation for Taxpayer and Consumer Rights wrote to the new governor demanding to know what transpired when he met Lay—the "biggest corporate crook in recent memory, while he and his firm were in the midst of ripping off the state," and why, having become governor, he called for dismantling the California Power Authority and renewed reliance on deregulated energy. Still, if Arnold groped in the right places, maybe the could win California in 2004!

THERMOSTATS SET FOR PROFITS

If Californians sweltered, maybe it was their fault. They had voted for Al Gore by a large margin. Since some Californians called for conservation, Bush gave it to them. On May 3, 2001, he ordered federal agencies in California to find ways to conserve power but gave no specific suggestions. Energy Secretary Spencer Abraham (whose political ambitions in Michigan had been fueled by Enron) said federal agencies would consider raising thermostats to 78 degrees and closing non-essential space.

While Enron traded energy, the leading producer of natural gas in the U.S. was British Petroleum, which had acquired both Amoco and Atlantic Richfield. On May 9, 2001, the chief executive of BP explained the company's recent high profits: "The trading environment remains broadly positive in spite of the slowdown in the world economy."

MEGAWATT LAUNDERING

On May 29, 2001, the Federal Energy Regulatory Commission (FERC) imposed price caps on electricity sold to California. Sellers of energy complained that the FERC caps distorted the markets. In October 2001, FERC ruled that four suppliers had overcharged California in July and ordered them to make partial refunds. After Enron declared bankruptcy on December 2, 2001, FERC obtained documents showing four techniques Enron used to manipulate prices in California:

(1) Creating and then "relieving" phantom congestion in the state's energy grid;

(2) "Death-star"—getting paid for moving energy to relieve congestion without moving or relieving anything;

(3) "Inc-ing load"—submitting unrealistic schedules into the state's real-time energy market; and,

(4) "Ricocheting"—megawatt laundering.[3]

"KENNY, I HARDLY KNEW YUH"

In January 2002, the Enron board asserted that it did not know about the firm's parlous finances until October 2001. Several years before, however, Enron's board had actually suspended the company's official code of ethics to approve the creation of partnerships between Enron and its chief financial officer. These arrangements kept huge debts off Enron's books and masked much of what was happening within the company.

But nobody knew nuthin'. Yep, Dubya knew Mr. Lay casually but didn't know much about Enron, even though it was his biggest source of campaign funding for years.[4] Lay and other Enron top execs didn't know that underlings cooked the books. Arthur Andersen accountancy didn't know either, 'cause it had nuthin' to go on but the data Enron provided. Andersen bigwigs in Chicago didn't know that Andersen employees at Enron HQ in Houston were shredding thousands of documents in the three months before Enron declared bankruptcy. The big banks and investment houses in New York that kept Enron afloat didn't know nuthin' either, 'cause they never got to see the real numbers. The little guys at the middle and lower ranks of Enron didn't know either. How could they guess what their bosses were up (or down) to?

HOW TO BUILD A NEST EGG:
LESSONS FROM ENRON

When Enron went belly-up, so did the retirement assets of many Enron employees—who had been forced to invest heavily in the company they worked for. In his January 2002, State of the Nation address, a compassionate President Bush called for better corporate disclosure and oversight of 401(k) retirement accounts. His long speech denounced the "axis of evil" but failed to mention Enron or campaign finance reform or Osama bin Laden or even the Middle East as a trouble spot.

House Minority Leader Dick Gephardt commented that campaign finance reform was needed to deal with undue political influence by firms such as Enron. "If the nation's largest bankruptcy isn't a prime case for reform, I don't know what is," said Gephardt.

HOW DE-REG CAN REGULATE FAMILY TIES

Senator Phil Gramm and his wife, Wendy, also worried about Enron-gate. When they danced, it was often to Enron's tune. A top recipient of Enron largesse, Gramm went all-out for deregulation. He helped win approval of a bill exempting energy commodity trading from government regulation and public disclosure. A member of President Reagan's task force on regulatory relief, Wendy later chaired the U.S. Commodity Futures Trading Commission, where she pushed through a ruling that exempted many energy futures contracts from regulation. Five weeks after she left the CFTC, she got a seat on Enron's board. From 1993 to 2001 she received more than a million dollars from Enron in salary, attendance fees, stock options and dividends.

Undaunted in his quest to twist the law for private gain, Gramm and other Senate Republicans continued in 2002 to resist Democratic moves to penalize U.S. firms that used offshore mail drops to avoid U.S. taxes. Gramm charged that Democrats were slapping business around because it was good politics.

Gramm's fellow Texan, Congressman Tom DeLay, also danced to Enron's tune. DeLay was known as "Dereg" in Austin.

SHOCKED TO THE PITT

Outraged! In 2002, both President Bush and Harvey Pitt, head of the Securities and Exchange Commission, expressed their displeasure when newspapers reported that executives at Enron, WorldCom and other leading companies cooked the books for personal gain while most of their employees, stockholders and the public suffered. The foxes promised to let no more chickens escape.

Dubya's choice to head the SEC was, well, the pitts. For years Pitt had been an attorney for many of the firms he was now to supervise. Taking on the job, Pitt promised a "kinder and gentler" SEC than in the Clinton years, when SEC boss Arthur Levitt crusaded for better corporate accounting.

In July 2002, Senator John McCain called for Pitt's resignation, because he had been slow to address accounting abuses. During his first ten months as SEC chairman, Pitt did not participate in 29 of the commission's votes, because most involved his former clients.

Even after the Enron disclosures, the Bush White House resisted calls to reform accounting procedures such as requiring firms to deduct the cost of executive stock options from reported profits. The Republican chairman of the House Financial Services Commission, Michael Oxley, became furious when the Merrill Lynch brokerage firm admitted having pushed stocks that its own analysts deemed worthless. He was angry—not because investors had been bilked—but because the company agreed to pay a fine. A long-time patron of the brokerage business, Oxley in 1995 had pushed though a law, over Bill Clinton's veto, blocking investor lawsuits.

SECRETS OF HORATIO ALGER
(MAKE SURE POPPY IS PREZ)

In Spring 2002, the Bush White House proposed that corporate officers be required to disclose sales of company stock within two days. But George W. had himself violated this rule in a big way. In 1989, he sat on the board of the Harken Energy Corporation after Harken paid $2 million for Spectrum 7, a money-losing energy firm headed by Dubya. But Harken was itself losing

big bucks. To cover its losses, Harken sold a subsidiary at a high price to Harken insiders who borrowed the purchase price from Harken! After the SEC caught on and ordered Harken to restate its 1989 earnings, Dubya sold two-thirds of his stake at $4 a share for $848,560. That was on June 22, 1990. Eight days later, Harken's accounting showed a quarterly loss of $23.2 million—eight times worse than the previous year. When the loss was publicly reported in August 1990, Harken stock fell to $2.37. Bush did not report his insider sale in June 1990, to the SEC until March 1991. An internal SEC memo concluded that George W. had broken the law because he failed to report this transaction promptly. But no charges were filed against a man whose father was then the U.S. president. Questioned in July 2002, the White House explained that Dubya's lawyers got "mixed up." The president told reporters that the issue had been "fully vetted. Any other questions?"

MARTHA STEWART BEFORE KENNETH LAY?

Faced with revelations that many big firms had inflated earnings and disguised losses, President Bush lectured Wall Street on the need for corporate responsibility. Some liberals doubted that Dubya's threat of heavy prison terms for errant executives would ever be enforced, while some conservatives said the president was being too harsh on those who made America's wheels hum. Columnist Paul Krugman asked (*New York Times*, May 10,

2002) why, if Bush was getting tough, he had not yet fired Secretary of the Army Thomas White, whose division at Enron had generated $500 million in phony profits and who sold $12 million in Enron stock just before the company collapsed? Attorney Sean Carter asked (www.counterpunch.com, June 3, 2003) why, instead of spending hours trying Martha Stewart, federal prosecutors did not pursue real criminals like the former heads of Enron and Adelphi University, as well as Carter's own stockbroker....

BLACK MARKS ON THE WHITE HOUSE

Enron penetrated the Bush team wide and deep. The Veep admitted that, as head of the Bush administration's energy task force, he had met several times with Enron's Ken Lay. U.S. Attorney General Ashcroft had to recuse himself from the Justice Department's Enron investigation because the company had donated nearly $61,000 to his failed 2000 senate campaign. Bush adviser Karl Rove was a major Enron stockholder when he met Lay to discuss Enron's problems with federal regulators. Bush's first secretary of the army, Thomas White, had worked for Enron for ten years. Former Montana Governor Marc Racicot was Enron's chief Washington lobbyist before being named national chairman of the Republican Party. U.S. Trade Representative Robert Zoelick had served on Enron's advisory council. Spencer Abraham,

Bush's first secretary of energy, took Enron contributions as a senator. At Lay's recommendation, Bush named Patrick H. Wood III, to chair the Federal Energy Regulatory Commission.[5]

HALLIBURTON MEANS COST-PLUS

In May 2002, the SEC opened an inquiry into the accounting practices of the oil services firm, Halliburton, headed by Cheney from 1995 to 2000. The SEC found that in 1998 Cheney had engineered the acquisition of a rival firm despite its asbestos liabilities. Halliburton shares appreciated and Cheney sold his holdings for nearly $40 million in mid 2000. When the full scale of the asbestos liabilities became known, however, Halliburton stock fell in July 2002 to one-third its value when Cheney unloaded his shares. Was Cheney stupid for not assessing the seriousness of the asbestos problems before the acquisition—or a knave for keeping them quiet until he bailed out? Or both?

Halliburton remained a major Pentagon contractor even as its former boss served as Dubya's VP and received more than $1 million each year from Halliburton in "deferred compensation." With Saddam gone, a Halliburton subsidiary, "KBR" (Kellogg, Brown & Root), received contracts to rebuild Iraq's oil industry and to provide U.S. military facilities. Audits

showed in December 2003 that KBR had overcharged the Pentagon $61 million for gasoline it imported from Kuwait and $67 million for dining halls built in Iraq. Meanwhile, Halliburton enjoyed an open-ended, "cost plus 1%" contract to provide U.S. base facilities from the Philippines to Yemen, as well as Iraq—an arrangement not calculated to minimize costs.

Chapter 4

THE DEMOCRACY MONEY CAN BUY

What is justice? One view is that might makes right. "What people call 'justice' is really just the interest of the stronger," said Thrasymachus, another character in Plato's *Republic*. Thrasymachus tells Socrates that a "so-called 'just' man will reward his backers and punish his enemies and in this way keep up his strength."

Socrates disagrees. He argues that "a just leader, like a good shepherd, will not look after his own personal interest, but that of his flock."

"You need a nursemaid," Thrasymachus tells Socrates, "if you fancy that the herdsman tends the sheep or cattle, fattening them up with a view to their good rather than his own or his master's good. Can't you see that a political leader sees his subjects precisely as cattle, and thinks of nothing else, day and night, but how to squeeze some advantage from them for himself."

To illustrate, Thrasymachus goes on: "Honest men always lose to dishonest. If a partnership goes bust, the unjust man always gets more and the just less. If the government imposes a tax, the just man will pay more and the unjust less on the same property.

Could the words of Thrasymachus, uttered 2,400 years ago, resonate (or "resignate," in the parlance of the U.S.'s 43rd president) in 21st century America? The answer, if we can believe Senator John McCain, is yes. The Arizona Republican told his fellow senators on March 19, 2001, that Americans had reason to believe that their elected representatives "would let this nation pay any price, and bear any burden, for the sake of securing our own ambitions, no matter how injurious the effect might be to the national interest."

DOES MONEY TALK? 2 x 1 = BUSH DEFEATS McCAIN

Beginning in 1995 Senators John McCain (R-Ariz.) and Russell Feingold (D-Wis.) introduced legislation meant to clean up campaign financing. They wanted to eliminate abuses of "soft money" donations by corporations,

unions, nonprofits, and individuals to political parties—often in the thousands or even millions of dollars. Soft money gifts were supposed to be spent only for party-building activities such as voter registration and turnout drives. In practice, however, soft money was often used to print or broadcast ads with a strong political message cloaked in the mantle of "public debate." Unlike soft money, hard money was subject to federal contribution limits set in 1974—ceilings of $1,000 per individual and $5,000 for each political action committee per election. Unlike soft money, hard money could be spent on ads explicitly seeking the election or defeat of a particular candidate.

In the contest to become Republican candidate in 2000, McCain spent $45 million and lost, while Bush won, having spent $110 million. The Arizona Republican gave Dubya only a lukewarm endorsement and continued his crusade against the corrupting influence of campaign donations. In January 2001, McCain demanded that the Republican-controlled Congress enact a campaign finance reform bill before it took up the new president's legislative agenda.

SHOULD MONEY TALK? THE SEDUCTION OF POWER

Many Democrats as well as Republicans resisted reform and sought to keep the gates open to soft money. Politics was big business. By the mid-1990s, Democrats were raising nearly as much soft money as Republicans. In 1995-1996, Republicans took in $141 million in soft money—about one-seventh

($19 million) more than Democrats. In 1999-2000, however, Democratic intake lagged Republican by just $1 million—$243 million versus $244 million. The real advantage for Republicans was in hard money. In 1995-1996, Republicans raked in nearly twice as much hard money as Democrats—$408 million versus $210 million. In 1999-2000, the gap narrowed but was still quite large: $447 million for Republicans versus $270 million for Democrats. Total donations to both parties ran to $881 million in 1995-1996 and to $1.2 billion in 1999-2000.

CAUGHT IN THE ACT

The Bipartisan Campaign Finance Reform Act, known as McCain-Feingold in the Senate, was co-sponsored by Representatives Christopher Shays (R-Conn.) and Martin T. Meehan (D-Mass.). Speaker of the House J. Dennis Hastert (R-Ill.) and Party Whip Tom DeLay (R-Tex.) worried how they could stop the bill's momentum, whipped along by public outrage over Enron and other scandals. Hastert, in his understated way, declared that the bill's passage would spell "Armageddon" for Republicans. Whip Tom DeLay saw the bill as "stepping all over the Bill of Rights, all over our freedom of speech, all over our freedom of association. It is not reform, it's incumbent protection."

DeLay pledged to "try anything I can" to scuttle the bill. But 41 Republicans joined with House Democrats on February 14, 2002, to approve the

reform law. The Senate also passed the bill, 60 to 40, and it was signed by President Bush on March 27, 2002.

The bill sought to close two loopholes in campaign finance law—"soft money" and "issue ads." It banned soft money donations to national political parties, but permitted donations (up to $10,000 per contributor) to state parties for voter registration and get-out-the-vote drives, while prohibiting their use to influence elections for Congress or president. The law set new

limits on what unions, corporations and nonprofit organizations could spend on issue ads and banned the use of such donations to sponsor "issue ads" referring to a specific candidate for federal office within 30 days of a primary and within 60 days of a general election. The law permitted hard money donations from individuals to rise from $1,000 to $2,000 for a particular candidate. Future hard money limits would be indexed to inflation. The act allowed individuals running against wealthy, self-financed candidates to receive triple the otherwise allowed hard-money contributions. The law would take effect on November 6, 2002, one day after mid-term elections but well before the next presidential election.

McCain argued that a ban on soft money would constrain the influence of big donors and increase the role of smaller contributors and regular voters. Cynics expected that soft money could still flow to interest groups with "shadow organizations" not technically linked to parties but ideologically tied to them.[1]

FORCED TO SIGN, FREE TO SKIRT

Instead of arranging a fancy signing ceremony for the new law, with photo ops for its sponsors, Bush dashed off his signature and then departed to solicit funds—whether hard or soft—still legal tender until after the November elections. At 7 a.m. Arizona time, a White House staffer phoned the senator who championed the bill to announce the accomplished fact. A presidential aid delivered to McCain's office a ceremonial pen wielded by the very man who sank his presidential hopes in their 2000 South Carolina face-off.

Bush's churlish behavior probably sought to mollify a right wing that foamed at the mouth over McCain's refusal to bow. Perhaps Bush also wanted to placate Attorney General Ashcroft, now obliged to defend reforms that he, as a senator, had staunchly opposed.

Meanwhile, the Federal Election Commission immediately moved to gut the McCain-Feingold law before it took effect on November 6, 2002. In June, the FEC ruled that (a) soft money could be used to finance Internet communications and (b) federal candidates could still solicit soft money for state parties and other allied groups. The FEC also eliminated any financial liability that parties might face for circumventing the law by creating independently run soft money conduits before November 6. McCain and the bill's other sponsors complained that the FEC was flouting congressional intent and substituting its own policy preferences. Even the FEC general counsel warned commissioners that some of their decisions had "the potential for great mischief."

Democracy 21, chaired by Fred Wertheimer, called for a completely new FEC structure. It argued that "the agency is a captive of the community it's supposed to be regulating."

At the same time, the Alliance for Better Campaigns, chaired by Jimmy Carter, Gerald Ford and Walter Cronkite, pushed for additional legislation to compel broadcast outlets to give candidates free air time—a common practice in Europe.

HARD MONEY AS FREE SPEECH

Texas Senator Phil Gramm (husband of an Enron board member) and Mitch McConnell (R-Ky.) had long fought against the campaign finance reforms. McConnell argued: "If people think money in politics is so pernicious, they should change the First Amendment" and its guarantee of free speech. Multimillionaire Senator Peter Fitzgerald (R-Ill.) chimed in: "The Supreme Court has said that spending one's own money in support of their candidacy is a constitutionally protected activity." Though Gramm and McConnell posed as defenders of the Constitution, some observers saw them as hypocrites.

Senator Mitch McConnell declared that the law created a new federal crime—"incitement to political action." He filed suit challenging the new law's constitutionality. More than 50 lawyers took up their cudgels, including Kenneth Starr, who had investigated the Clintons for years, spending millions. A coalition of strange bedfellows also filed complaints: the

National Rifle Association, the Christian Coalition, AFL-CIO, U.S. Chamber of Commerce, American Civil Liberties Union and the Republican National Committee—even though a Republican president had signed the law. They complained that McCain-Feingold violated their right to free speech, even though political ads could still be financed by hard money.

The case known as McConnell, *et al.* v. Federal Election Commission, *et al.* went first to a three-judge panel of the D.C. District Court, which struck down 9 of 20 challenged provisions. On appeal, however, the Supreme Court, by 5 to 4 vote, in December 2003 upheld most provisions of the law. The court rejected claims the law violated the First Amendment, affirming the authority of Congress to act against the corrupting power of money in politics. The court minority argued that the law violated free speech and was unnecessary, since there was no real corruption in the present system—no trading of money for favors.[2]

The decision gave an advantage to candidates such as President Bush and Howard Dean, adept at raising the smaller, regulated donations known as "hard money." Tapping hard money sources, Bush had already collected $100 million in 2003; Dean, exploiting the Internet, more than $25 million—far more than other Democrats.

"ALL POWER GROWS FROM THE BARREL OF A GUN":
MAO ZEDONG AND THE NRA

"We ought to keep guns out of the hands of people that shouldn't have them," George W. declared in May 2000. Candidate Dubya denied he was a tool of the National Rifle Association even though the NRA gave him strong support. As president, Bush did budget for free trigger locks on guns but otherwise threw his weight behind NRA causes.

The Bush team found a constitutional right it wanted to expand! Mr. Ashcroft told the NRA in 2001 that, "the text and original intent of the Second Amendment clearly protect the right of individuals to keep and bear firearms." The U.S. Solicitor General made the same pitch to the Supreme Court in May 2002. This interpretation broke from both precedent and policy established in 1939 when the court ruled that the Second Amendment aimed to ensure the effectiveness of a "well-regulated militia"—not to guarantee an individual's right to bear firearms.

The NRA Political Victory Fund invested many millions backing opponents of gun control in the November 2002, elections. When the Supreme Court upheld McCain-Feingold, the NRA deliberated whether to purchase its own TV and radio stations as a way to skirt limits on issue ads a month or two before elections. The finance campaign law permitted news organizations to broadcast on issues like gun control if not owned by political party, committee or candidate.

SUBSIDIES FOR MANURE CLEANUP

As the war on terrorism and tax cuts widened the federal budget, Congress in May 2002, rammed through new subsidies for agriculture. The cartoon shows only half the picture, because the pork was bipartisan. Senate Majority Leader Tom Daschle (D-S.Dak.) termed the law "a good, constructive, forward-looking bill." It raised price guarantees for corn, wheat, oats and sorghum and also revived a target price system for additional payments to farmers when commodity prices fell below certain levels. Individual farms could receive as much as $210,000 a year through the direct-payment and target-price programs. Over ten years, the package would boost agriculture spending by 70%, or $73.5 billion, according to *The Morning Sun* in Pittsburgh, Kansas.

Here was something for nearly everybody—new subsidies for dairy farmers as well as producers of lentils, chickpeas, honey, wool, mohair and apples. Owners of peanut quotas would receive 11 cents a pound annually for five years. Sugar producers would no longer be required to pay a penny-per-pound penalty when they forfeited sugar pledged as collateral. The conservation program paying farmers to idle environmentally sensitive land would be expanded to cover more acreage. Inducements to farmers near urban areas to keep their land in production would expand by nearly $1 billion over the decade, a roughly 20-fold increase. Subsidies for manure cleanup and other environmental improvements would jump by $9 billion. Non-citizens in the U.S. for five years would become eligible for food stamps, but many imported foods would have to be labeled with their country of origin.

SWARMY INCEST

Close relatives of three top members of Congress worked as lobbyists in 2002. Joshua Hastert, 27, eldest son of House Speaker J. Dennis Hastert; Chester T. Lott, Jr., son of the Senate Republican Leader Trent Lott; and Linda Daschle, 47, wife of the Senate Majority Leader Tom Daschle. As reported in *The New York Times* on August 4, 2002, Joshua's pierced tongue and goatee, as well as his previous job as owner of a record label called Seven Dead Arson, set him apart from the typical buttoned-down Washington lobbyist. Such connections were not illegal, but were they ethical? "Why should a spouse, just because she is married to a high-profile public official, have to walk away from a career?" asked Mrs. Daschle. "It is the swarminess and incestuousness that is most objectionable," said Charles Lewis, director of the Center for Public Integrity.

THE OMEGA AND ALPHA OF EVIL

The system's capacity for corruption was manifest in Richard Perle, long known in D.C. as the "Prince of Darkness." An assistant defense secretary under President Reagan, but now a private citizen, Perle chaired Secretary Rumsfeld's Defense Policy Board, where he could advance his business as well as his pro-Israeli agendas. Not only was Perle a director of the Autonomy Corporation, a manufacturer of eavesdropping equipment for the Department of Homeland Security, but he was also a lobbyist for Global Crossing as it tried to sell itself to a Chinese consortium—a technology transfer that FBI and Pentagon experts believed dangerous to national security. When these conflicts of interests surfaced in March 2003, Perle resigned the chair but remained on the Defense Policy Board. All hell broke loose in December 2003, after Perle touted the merits of the Pentagon's $20 billion lease (instead of purchase) of 100 refueling planes from Boeing in *The Wall Street Journal* without revealing that Boeing was investing up to $20 million in Trireme Partners, Perle's venture capital firm. Boeing denied any wrongdoing: It had merely briefed Perle in his capacity as a fellow at the American Enterprise Institute, a think tank much admired by George W. Bush. Smelling several skunks, the Pentagon suspended its tanker deal and the CEO of Boeing resigned. Unfazed by accusations of multiple conflicts of interests, Perle joined with David Frum (retired speech writer who gave us the "axis-of-evil") to advise Americans how to achieve "an end to evil."[3] Having served on the defense policy board for 17 years, Perle resigned in February 2004, saying he didn't want his controversial views to be attributed to President Bush in an election year.

Barbara Walters: "Isn't it all—so much of it—about oil? Shouldn't we be changing our energy policy?"
Bush: "The war on terror has nothing to do about oil."

George W. Bush
December 13, 2002

Chapter 5

GREEN OR BLACK? THE WEIGHT OF BIG COAL AND BIG OIL

"You've got to ask the question," George W. Bush declared in May 1999, "is the air cleaner since I became governor? And the answer is yes."

Machiavelli's "answer" was a bald lie. U.S. Environmental Protection Agency data showed that air pollution in Texas increased by 11% under Governor Bush. Texas spewed out more toxins and carcinogens than any other state. Governor George W. stacked the state environmental agency with spokesmen for industry and agriculture who lobbied—not for clean air but against federal regulations enacted in 1997. Working with big chemical and energy producers, Governor Bush enacted a law providing for voluntary compliance with pollution standards. The very firms that helped design this law donated heavily to Bush's gubernatorial campaign in 1998 and to his presidential campaign in 2000. Houston replaced Los Angeles in 1999 as the U.S. city with the most dangerous smog. In 2000, Texas ranked 46th among states in water-resources protection. School children in Texas, as we shall see in the next chapter, were told not to worry if the world became warmer.

As Texas suffered, so would the entire country—indeed, the entire planet—when Mr. Bush became president. President George W. called for self-regulation by industry and fought government regulations to maintain environmental quality. The Bush team torpedoed or put off for many years rules that would force manufacturers to produce more fuel-efficient trucks, sports utility vehicles and air conditioners. Few Americans realize that Europeans and the Japanese enjoy living standards similar to U.S. while burning far less energy.

Instead of leading the country toward less dependence on oil and coal, Bush nurtured the belief that Americans have a God-given right to speed along vast highways in huge gas-guzzlers. While some SUV owners claimed that they paid for their gasoline and others should shut up, the true costs of America's gas guzzling are borne by every being on the planet. Besides economic and environmental burdens, Americans wrestle with the results of Washington's ties to oil-rich sheikdoms and U.S. efforts to dominate oil-rich regions from the Caspian Sea to Nigeria and Ecuador.

FOXES AND LIONS TO GUARD CHICKENS

Taking office in 2001, Bush named Gail Norton to be secretary of the interior. As attorney general in Colorado, she had disputed the constitutionality of many environmental protection laws and contended that property owners

should be compensated if federal regulations decreased the value of their land. "We might even go so far as to recognize a homesteading right to pollute," she wrote. Did this passionate libertarian really believe in stewardship of federal lands—the job to which she was appointed?

Bush named Christine Todd Whitman to head the Environmental Protection Agency (EPA). Her appointment drew cheers from the chemical industry, quite comfortable when she governed New Jersey and abolished the enforcement arm of the state's environmental agency.

Bush named Spencer Abraham to be secretary of energy. Recently defeated in his bid for reelection as senator from Michigan, Abraham had close ties to automakers opposed to fuel efficiency rules. As a senator, Abraham had called for eliminating the Energy Department he was now to head. As a senator, Abraham received a grade of zero from the League of Conservation Voters—as did John Ashcroft, now the Attorney General supposed to enforce the country's laws.

FULL STEAM

How often at night when the heavens are bright
With the light of the glittering stars,
Have I stood here amazed and asked as I gazed
If their glory exceeds that of ours.

Did Bush want the whole country, like Texas, to become more black than green? He declared in March 2001, that America was in the midst of an

energy crisis and so should not regulate carbon dioxide emissions by
power plants—undercutting EPA Administrator Whitman who in February had promoted Bush's previous vow to reduce carbon dioxide emissions
in partnership with other countries. But cheers came from power utilities
and the coal-mining industry that helped deliver to Bush the traditionally
Democratic state of West Virginia in 2000. Did not Bush in September 2000,
offer unqualified support for regulating CO^2? Staffers replied in 2001 that
the president had just learned carbon dioxide is not classified as a pollutant
under the Clean Air Act.

Having heard from Dick Cheney's energy task force, the White House
asked in 2001 for a new power plant every week for the next twenty years,
ignoring energy efficiency measures that government scientists said could
cut demand by 20 to 47% in coming years. Cheney allowed that conservation may be virtuous, but denied it a major role in public policy. The Bush
budget for 2004 reduced government funding for conservation research by
8%.

>*Oh, give me a land where the bright diamond sand*
>*Flows leisurely down the stream*
>*Where the graceful white swan goes gliding along*
>*Like a maid in a heavenly dream.*

In March 2001, EPA Administrator Whitman revoked Clinton-era rules
that would reduce arsenic in Americans' drinking water so as to meet World
Health Organization standards within five years. Ms. Whitman stated that
the EPA would devise new, more reasonable standards that imposed a lighter

economic burden and were based more on science than those being dismantled. Meanwhile, 34 million Americans were drinking water with elevated
levels of arsenic occurring naturally or as a result of pollution—with the
biggest problems in the Southwest, Midwest and Northeast. Persons leery
of arsenic and other pollutants had to pay more for bottled water than for
gasoline.[1]

NO TREES, NO FIRES

When the president stopped for a photo shoot at Sequoia National Park in
June 2001, he painted himself in green. He delivered a 12-minute pep talk
calling for outlays of $5 billion over the next five years to repair national
parks. He talked as if this were a new initiative, though some funding was already in place and other funds would come from not buying new parklands.

Using Orwellian double-speak, Dubya in August 2002, promoted a
"Healthy Forest" plan calling for laws to "expedite procedures for forest thinning and restoration" and "ensure the sustainable forest management and appropriate timber production." To reduce "unnecessary regulatory obstacles,"
Bush wanted to make it easier for loggers to thin out backcountry forests
and to make it harder for environmentalists to stop or delay that work. In
December 2003, the president signed the Healthy Forests Restoration Act, a
law the White House claimed would reduce the complexity of environmental

analysis used to manage public lands. One example it gave was the Pillsbury Homesites in California's Mendocino National Forest, a project "designed to remove understory through commercial thinning, followed by mechanical treatment (in this case, dozer piling of small material)...."

The Bush administration also acted to exempt the Tongass National Forest in Alaska, the largest in the country, from a Clinton-era rule, potentially opening up more than half of the 17-million acre forest for more development and logging.

"D" FOR DISASTERS

More green paint was splashed as the chief executive darted from California to Florida. Bush had major incentives to please Floridians. Their votes had been and could again be decisive in national elections. Also, Dubya wanted to help his brother Jeb, governor of Florida. But many Floridians were upset that Interior Secretary Gale Norton had notified Governor Jeb in March 2001, that she planned to proceed with a proposal to auction oil and gas development leases in a large tract in the eastern Gulf of Mexico—some of it within 30 miles of the Florida Panhandle. Governor Jeb's backers applauded when brother George later got the federal government to buy back oil leases in the eastern Gulf of Mexico and the Everglades. But several oil companies still had a foot in the door and might drill in Florida waters at a later date.

Why shield Florida but push to drill in Alaska's Arctic National Wildlife Refuge and offshore California? The president said his decisions were made case-by-case and that local interests and economic factors influenced his decision to protect the Sunshine State.

Floridians responded favorably when, following a hike in the Everglades National Park, George W. declared in June 2001, that he would continue the federal government's commitment to improve Everglades water quality, storage and flow. The commitment, made under Clinton, was to split with Florida estimated costs of $8 billion, spread over 40 years. But initial outlays for Everglades restoration were minuscule. Bush's 2002 budget called for $219 million spread over five federal agencies. Despite an uptick in Bush's green-speak, the National Parks and Conservation Association gave him a grade of D for his commitment to the parks.

SOME LIKE IT HOT

In 1997, the Clinton Administration signed the Kyoto protocol to reduce emissions of greenhouse gases. When Clinton left office, the Senate still had not approved the treaty. But President Bush flat-out repudiated the treaty as unnecessary, too expensive and too weak. Trying to explain, he said on April 24, 2001: "First, we would not accept a treaty that would not have been ratified, nor a treaty that I thought made sense for the country."

Bush questioned whether global warming was taking place and, if so, whether human actions played a key role. Dubya objected that Kyoto required industrialized countries to reduce emissions of suspected "greenhouse" gases but placed no specific curbs on less developed countries.

The White House later said it was concerned about global warming and would propose other ways to deal with it. In 2002-2003, however, it did little more than promote voluntary restraints by industry that would at most slow the increase in the rate of carbon emissions relative to growth in GDP (gross domestic product). Meanwhile, the administration struggled to open new lands and sea beds to oil exploration, while Congress refused to tighten fuel efficiency standards for sports-utility and most other vehicles.

Washington encouraged Americans to buy gas-guzzlers—the heavier and costlier the better—and they did. Owners of light trucks weighing more than 6,000 pounds could deduct up to $100,000 a year from tax liability. Such vehicles faced few, if any, penalties for exceeding the fuel consumption limits imposed on lighter cars. Detroit, followed by Subaru, responded by transforming station wagons into "light trucks" (aka SUVs). The Bush team proposed tightening limits on fuel consumption by some light trucks in 2004, but the effect would be neutralized by other loopholes in the law. Purchasers of battery powered hybrids got only minuscule tax write-offs.

"O BEAUTIFUL FOR SPACIOUS SKIES"

Not long after the president rejected Kyoto, the U.S. National Academy of Sciences reported on June 7, 2001, that greenhouse gases were indeed accumulating as a result of human activities and causing surface temperatures to rise. Glaciers were retreating, Arctic ice thinning, sea levels rising and warm seasons lengthening. Decisions taken now, the report said, would influence the extent of damage suffered later in the century. National Security Advisor Condoleezza Rice, however, tried to spin the report. She observed that the president took climate change very seriously and would discuss it soon with European leaders, noting that the Europeans and the U.S. did not always agree. She added that Washington would continue to insist that Third World countries be included in any plan to halt global warming.

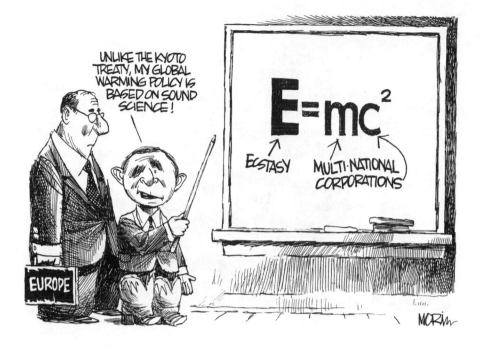

DAMN THE BUREAUCRACY, FULL SPEED AHEAD!

"I don't think we know the solution to global warming yet. And I don't think we've got all the facts before we make decisions...."—GWB quoted in *The Boston Globe*, June 7, 2002.

Drawing on a recent study by the National Academy of Sciences, the EPA reported in June 2002, that global warming was already affecting the U.S. in significant ways and that human activities played a decisive role in bringing on these trends. The president who occasionally joked about his poor academic record dismissed this as another report by the federal "bureaucracy"—probably the best science available.

Despite the many cataclysmic changes forecast, the Bush team argued that any problems caused by global warming could be met by adaptation. The White House pledged only to lower the greenhouse intensity of U.S. economic activity (the level of emissions per unit of economic output) by 18% from 2002 to 2012. This would reduce U.S. emissions by 4.5% from what would otherwise be their level in 2012. Thus, America's total emissions would increase, but the U.S. would pollute less for every unit of GDP. This "reduction" would be achieved by a "combination of voluntary, incentive-based and existing mandatory measures." In 2003, Russia followed Bush's example and refused to ratify the Kyoto protocol, leaving it in limbo or dead.

CRAWFORD, Da; YELLOWSTONE, Nyet

Dubya bought the 1,600-acre Crawford, Texas, ranch when he was governor. Bushland was less than 8 miles on the Prairie Chapel Road from Crawford's only traffic light. As president, Bush usually arrived by helicopter, but he did not much ruffle the pastoral ways of this metropolis of 700 souls. In August 2001, Mr. Bush told reporters: "I've seen fox here, I've seen all kinds of birds. It's a wonderful spot to come up in here and just kind of think about the budget." A year later, in August 2002, hawks swooped in at the ranch to deliberate what to do about Iraq. Dovish connoisseurs of white wine (Colin Powell?) were relegated to Martha's Vineyard or the Hamptons. Bush soul-mates such as Tony B. and Vladimir P., however, were honored guests from time to time.

Meanwhile, the president revoked a Clinton-era ban on snowmobiles chugging through Yellowstone and Grand Teton national parks, "where the deer and the antelope play," compelling Park Rangers once again to don gas masks and cross-country skiers to cough. When a U.S. District Court ordered the ban restored in 2003, Interior Secretary Gale Norton protested. Soon, a local court ordered a "compromise" allowing hundreds of snowmobiles into the park each day. Again, the fumes and sounds of these machines mixed with the spray of Old Faithful, the breath of bison, and the crackling of ice.

"FOR PURPLE MOUNTAIN MAJESTIES
ABOVE THE FRUITED PLAIN!"

The Bush administration announced in May 2002, that it would relax Clinton-era rules and permit mining companies to blast the tops off mountains to get at coal—even though the resulting waste would fill valleys, streams and wetlands. But coal-mining companies often did not bother to get Clean Water Act permits to "clean-and-dredge" before filling in valleys. One EPA study in 2003 found more than 275 mining operations that illegally buried streams in West Virginia, Ohio and Kentucky. In late 2003, despite such signs of bad faith, the Bush team planned to allow coal companies to police their own mountaintop removal activities. The EPA's Mountaintop Mining Self-Reporting Program would assess a small fine for those companies that reported their own violations—another step toward complete deregulation and destruction of entire ecosystems across Appalachia.

"Superfund Gets the Super Shaft," said *Time* on February 25, 2002, as the White House junked the "polluter must pay" principle. The administration designated 33 toxic waste sites in 18 states for cuts in financing under the Superfund cleanup program. Unburdening chemical and mining industries, Republicans wanted to shift the burden to the tax-paying public. The White

House "seems determined to weaken the rules we are trying to enforce," said Eric Schaeffer, a top EPA enforcement officer, when he resigned in February 2002.

In 2002, soon after Schaeffer left office, the Bushies also relaxed regulations on older coal-fired furnaces, despite a study by Abt Associates predicting that 80 power plants owned by eight electric utilities would cause nearly 6,000 premature deaths by 2007—550 just in Pennsylvania—and 140,000 asthma attacks. All eight companies had been cited by the Justice Department for violating the Clean Air Act, but were contesting the charges. The EPA now halted many of its suits, however, because the alleged violations had become legal. The EPA moved to cut staff and drastically reduce its enforcement efforts. In the first three years of the Bush presidency, federal prosecution of clean air and water violations fell by 40%.

In February 2003, the Bush team submitted its "Clear Skies" initiative to Congress. The legislation set weaker targets for controlling emissions than those which would have been put in place if existing law were implemented. The Bush plan, for example, would allow three times more toxic mercury emissions, 50% more sulfur and hundreds of thousands more tons of smog-forming nitrogen oxides. In December 2003, a federal appeals court blocked the new rule to weaken existing law governing pollution from power plants and other industrial facilities.[2]

Senators Joseph L. Lieberman and John McCain complained in July 2003, that the EPA was refusing even to analyze their proposals to reduce carbon emissions. Lieberman complained: "This is an administration that lets its politics and ideology overwhelm and stifle scientific fact."[3]

The dangers of under-regulation were highlighted by the emergence of mad cow disease in Washington State. Some feared also that Alisa Harrison, spokesperson for the Department of Agriculture, might swallow her tongue. In her previous role as PR director for the National Cattlemen's Beef Association, Harrison had criticized Oprah Winfrey for raising health questions about hamburgers, and had sent out press releases with titles like "Mad Cow Disease: Not a Problem in the U.S." The Bush team had placed many foxes such as Ms. Harrison to guard the nation's chicken coops. Eric Schlosser, author of *Fast Food Nation*, doubted that any federal agency could match Agriculture for penetration by reps of the industry it was supposed to regulate, such as a former president of the National Pork Producers Council. In early 2004, when a beef exporter in Kansas wanted to test all of its cattle for mad cow disease to regain access to Japanese markets, the Department of Agriculture balked. How dare anyone hint that its existing standards were insufficient?

Chapter 6

MIND CONTROL: DRILL AND KILL

Education comes from the Latin for "lead out" or "bring up." But passionate conservatives seek mind control. In the 1990s, as we saw in Chapter 1, George H.W. Bush paid homage to a master brainwasher, Reverend Moon. But passionate conservatives in Texas also had powerful methods. The Texas Public Policy Foundation pressured the State Board of Education to adopt only textbooks that promoted democracy, patriotism and free enterprise. The State Board rejected textbooks criticized as "anti-technology," "anti-Christian," and "anti-American." It discouraged depictions of white settlers as rapacious toward Native Americans or nature.

To obtain a place on the state's "conforming list," publishers replaced warnings about global warming with reassurances that the earth had been warmer in previous times. "So does it really matter if the world gets warmer?" Many publishers frothed to get a piece of the state's textbook adoptions—worth more than $600 million just for history and social sciences. Holt, Rinehart & Winston and Pearson Prentice Hall, among others, thanked the Texas Public Policy Foundation for guidance that improved their offerings. But René LeBel, publisher of an approved text in environmental science, called the review process "a book burning...100% political." [1]

The Texas State Board of Education encouraged schools to bolster students' "constitutional right of voluntary, noncoercive prayer and ... to express their feelings of faith and patriotism."

The guardians in Plato's Republic also used education to promote mind control and social cohesion, but they renounced any quest for personal wealth. Dubya and his brothers, unlike Plato's guardians, used their political and economic leverage in education, as in other realms, to upgrade their fortunes.

Virtue, learning, and money go together for the preeminent Republican educator-moralist, William J. Bennett, Secretary of Education under President Reagan and drug czar for President Bush the elder. Bennett's many books range from *The Book of Virtues* to *Why We Fight: Moral Clarity and the War on Terrorism*. Here is a contemporary Tartuffe (described in the

next chapter). Never one to pass up giving a sermon and scoring a profit at
the same time, Bennett founded "K12," a firm that sells at-home learning
packages over the Internet (noted by some for their "white Anglo-Saxon"
approach to history). Bennett's Web site: www.empoweramerica.org, pro-
motes not only his writings but also explains how stock options for Enron
and other executives serve the public weal. When not kneeling in prayer,
Bennett chairs Americans for Victory Over Terrorism and plays the slots.
Washington Monthly (June 2003) estimated this "bookie of virtue" (said also
to write or edit speeches for Dubya) has lost more than $8 million at late-
night casinos in Vegas and New Jersey, where he has listed his address as
that of Empower America. Since Bennett pulls in some $50k per morality
lecture, however, his habit has not yet put him in the poor house. Though
not excusing Bennett's gambling habit, a *National Review* contributor said it
might arise from biology and, whatever the source, did less harm than Jessie
Jackson's fathering an illegitimate child.

MANY CHILDREN LEFT BEHIND

Under Governor Bush, Texas ranked near the bottom of all states in helping children break from poverty and ignorance. Child and teen deaths, along with teen dropouts and truancies, were much higher than the national average. Levels of child poverty stabilized across most of the U.S. in the 1990s but grew worse in Texas. Glossing over his record in Texas, George W. vowed in 2000 that, if elected president, "no child will be left behind (NCLB)." However, Al Gore's Tennessee also placed near the bottom in education and child protection—a rank it maintained while Harvard-grad Gore served as congressman, senator, and vice president. Given the sad performance of Tennessee and Texas under Gore and Bush, neither could do more than ask voters to admire his bright ideas for the future.

Of course it was implausible that anyone with Dubya's academic record, simplistic worldview, linguistic shortcomings and manifest lack of curiosity would claim any competence to evaluate any approach to education. Still, he touted a "Houston model" of accountability developed under Rod Paige, an ex-football coach, who became Houston's superintendent of education and thence Dubya's secretary of education.

REACHING FOR MINIMAL SKILLS IN TEXAS

The Houston model turned out to be a scam. A front-page analysis in *The New York Times*, December 3, 2003, demonstrated that the rapid progress shown by Houston pupils on the Texas Assessment of Academic Skills (TAAS) in the late 1990s was all smoke and mirrors. When 75,000 Houston pupils took the Stanford Achievement Test, which permitted comparisons across states, it turned out that, after several years, the city's 4th and 8th graders had improved very little while 10th graders failed the Stanford test.

In 2003, Texas officials admitted that the TAAS tested only "minimal skills" and needed upgrading. Scores were boosted by keeping many special ed and pupils with "limited English" from taking the test (as did North Carolina—see note 3). Further inflating the Houston model, local principals undercounted truancy, dropouts and serious crime in schools, while overstating the number of college-ready and college-bound students.

The NCLB law signed by President Bush in January 2002 gave public schools across the U.S. twelve years to match Houston's success and bring all children to academic proficiency. But in schooling, as in clean air, Houston showed how *not* to proceed.

UNDERFUNDED MANDATES

The NCLB law emphasized "accountability for results." To receive federal money for their schools, states had to set challenging standards in reading and mathematics and develop statewide annual adequate yearly progress (AYP) objectives that resulted in all groups of students achieving proficiency within 12 years. These objectives had to be met by all groups of students, disaggregated by poverty, race and ethnicity, disability and limited English proficiency. States had to conduct annual reading and math assessments for all students in grades 3-8, and states, school districts and schools had to make annual progress reports. Every two years a sample of each state's pupils would have to take part in the National Assessment of Educational Progress (NAEP), a federally mandated test known as the "nation's report card," to gauge the rigor of state standards and assessments.

Providing a "standards-based" NCLB education for all children would require new investments in education—from 15% to 50% or more per state. But debt-ridden states were shortchanged by the federal budget. In 2002, Congress appropriated only $11.3 billion for remedial education under Title 1—one-third less than the $18 billion authorized in NCLB. But President Bush requested only $12.3 billion for 2003, saying that the additional $1 billion was "more than enough money" and that "we are insisting that schools use that money wisely." [2] This one billion was about 1/200th of the cost of invading and rebuilding Iraq in 2003-2004, without adding in death and veterans benefits.

The disconnect between mandated progress and federal funding stirred a revolt by many school districts in 2003-2004. The front page of *The New York Times*, January 2, 2004, reported that a "growing number of school systems around the country are beginning to resist the demands of President Bush's signature education law, saying its efforts to raise student achievement are too costly and too cumbersome." Some Utah Republicans regarded the NCLB Act as an "unfunded mandate." Some districts were returning federal money to Washington rather than comply with federal red tape or cough up the money locally to meet federal rules. Some Republicans from the National Council of States Legislatures went straight to the White House to complain that the law violates states' rights. An outstanding school in Connecticut would have been penalized, if it accepted federal money, because only 94.3% of its students took a math test rather the required 95%. The school system in Reading, Pennsylvania, considered filing suit against the federal government because its schools got too little money to cope with an influx of students needing tutoring in English at a time of local economic distress.

DO STICKS WORK BETTER
THAN CARROTS?

The centerpiece of NCLB is high-stakes testing—the requirement that test scores improve annually. This approach ignores the danger that a single quantitative measure to show improvement in learning is bound to distort and corrupt the whole endeavor. Drill can kill. Teaching to the test could readily weaken America's unique advantage—its creativity. Science, as well as the arts, requires intuition as well as reason. Creativity is "feel/think"—not "fact-spout." Bright ideas inspire the best research.

Gifted pupils are bored by tests aimed at lifting the common denominator. Asked what she thought of the multiplying rounds of testing in her Lexington, Massachusetts, school, fourth-grader Annie Rosa says she hates them. "Teachers are pressing kids to learn by reviewing last year's exams." Annie prefers to apply what she had learned in different subjects to an exam question she has never seen before.

Mark Edmundson, author of *Teacher*, says teachers are now tasked to prepare students for "fact-based tests, to stuff our charges with information, like Christmas birds." Edmundson recalls a high school teacher, short and oddly dressed, who created a classroom atmosphere in which a student could say virtually anything and be sure of being accepted. This teacher shared what he loved and helped students to love and learn. Could a teacher do all that and also teach to the test?

Negative sanctions discourage learning. A comparison of states using high-stakes testing with other states showed little or no carry-over to real learning from high-stakes tests. Even more striking, all the high-stakes states (such as Texas) began and ended with lower SAT (Scholastic Aptitude Test) scores than states that had so far avoided high-stakes tests. High-stakes testing did not conduce to higher rates of high school completion or college attendance.[3]

Undermining the high-stakes testing even further, tests differ from state to state. Within a single state, more than half of the year-to-year change in test scores for grade levels or schools is simply random variation. The particular assembly of pupils and teachers changes each year. So do graders and standards. Readers make mistakes when fatigued. Machines also err. Often they are programmed with the wrong answers, with the result that students flunk when they should have passed.

SUFFER THE CHILDREN

In 2000 candidate Bush purloined the slogan "no child left behind" from the Children's Defense Fund, only to leave behind in 2001-2004 much of the Fund's campaign to boost pre-school education and assure health care for America's eleven million children without health insurance. In February 2002, Bush called for cuts in funds for local preschool tutoring, literacy efforts and school construction.

Early in 2002, Secretary of Health and Human Services Tommy Thomson announced insurance coverage for zygotes and other pre-born beings. For beings born to poor parents, however, it might be safer to remain in the womb. The Bush budget called for yearly cuts in funding for teaching hospitals and in medical training at hospitals specializing in children's health. Also Bush-whacked were funds for public housing, community development, heating subsidies, occupational safety and health, and job training. Or, instead of staying in the womb, poor kids might follow the advice of Stephanie Salter (*San Francisco Chronicle*, February 6, 2002) and turn themselves into an F-22 jet or Hellfire missile funded by the Pentagon's $70 billion procurement budget.

POTEMKIN ALTERNATIVES

Pupils from disadvantaged backgrounds are often turned off by tests that underscore their weakness—witness the higher dropout rates in some schools in the first years of NCLB. The gap between America's highest- and lowest-scoring students is larger than in any other industrialized country. This gap reflects a huge and growing chasm between rich and poor Americans—exacerbated by tax relief for the wealthy few and no jobs or minimum-wage jobs for the many. Pupils in poor neighborhoods get less support at home and in school than those in affluent districts.

The threat to schools in poor neighborhoods to "improve test scores or shut down" was unlikely to help. To raise standards as NCLB envisions would require a huge infusion of money, but in 2002-2003 Congress and the president raised existing funding by only a few percentage points. The first-year increases to Title I compensatory funds amounted to a mere 0.4% of total education spending. The "flexibility" procedures allowed by NCLB allowed local districts to shift around less than 5% of its already-committed money.

When some pupils tried to shift to other schools, they found "no vacancy" signs. The alternative schools for pupils who do not improve are Potemkin façades—few exist in the real world.

On February 23, 2004, Education Secretary Paige did not endear himself to many teachers when he called the National Education Association a "terrorist organization" that engages in "obstructionist scare tactics." Offended that their complaints about NCLB would be depicted in this way, the N.E.A. asked the White House to fire the Houston poster child.

LET THEM EAT CAKE

"First, it's arsenic in the water. Now it's salmonella in school lunches. Where will this end?" asked Senator Richard J. Durbin (D-Ill.). In April 2001, the Bush team prepared to tear down another rule set by the Clinton administration to protect public health—a requirement that ground beef used in school lunches be tested for salmonella by the U.S. Department of Agriculture. The inspections were mandated in June 2000, after a Texas meat-processing plant failed salmonella tests three times. Between then and March 2001, nearly one in ten samples of meat failed the tests—60% of them because of salmonella; the others because of e-coli or other problems.

Salmonella causes 1.4 million illnesses and 600 deaths a year, according to the Centers for Disease Control and Prevention. The Bush team proposed to destroy both salmonella and e-coli by irradiating meat. Meat packers welcomed this approach. But the uproar from consumers was so intense that the White House rescinded the proposed changes within hours. Bush's handlers could not welcome another fiasco like that after the Reagan administration classified catsup and relish as vegetables in school lunch programs. Several years later, the dangers of not testing more cattle for mad cow disease hit the front pages.

The president denounced the use of steroids in sports in his 2004 State of the Union address, but his diplomats continued to block efforts by the World Health Organization to advertise the risks of smoking, publicize the fat content of food and deliver affordable drugs for HIV, tuberculosis and other ailments. Deaths caused by tobacco and obesity in the U.S. and worldwide were millions of times greater than those caused by SARS or bird flu, but tobacco and corn syrup lobbyists carried great weight in Washington.

MUSICAL ROBOTS

One hand washes the other in the Bush dynasty: Dubya mandates, Jeb sponsors and Neil sells—exploiting both family name and capital.[4] When brother George pushed NCLB, Neil took money from his parents and Michael Millken (yes, the same fraudster who met Ken Lay and Arnold in California) and formed a company to sell teaching machinery. One way to leave no child behind, Neil suggested, was to brighten the attention-deficited with music and pictures. Neil's firm, "Ignite! Learning" enlivened historical documents such as the Articles of Confederation with a hip-hop beat and animation. Ignite!'s Web site describes its Federation Jingle: "An [sic] parody of early radio commercials [from the 1780s?], this piece combines humor with a catchy musical refrain to teach the complex idea of federalism in a concise and memorable way." One history lesson went like this: "It was 55 delegates from 12 states / Took one hot Philadelphia summer to create / A perfect document for their imperfect times / Franklin / Madison / Washington / A lot of cats / Who used to be in the Continental Congress way back."

Ignite! courseware aligns with each state's standards. Test runs began in Texas, Florida and four other states. Since two of the school boards courted by Neil were employees in a state currently or previously governed by one of his brothers, business prospects were good. Rod Paige came from D.C. to speak at the same conference of Florida educators with Neil. Ignite!'s

wares sold like hotcakes—even at $30 per student. Investors from Saudi
Arabia and the United Arab Emirates joined in the fun. China's President
Jiang Zemin threw a dinner and sang for the Texas entrepreneur.[5]

Ignite!, like William Bennett's K12 home-learning packages, capitalized
on the campaign to improve U.S. schooling. Bennett connected education
with U.S. intervention in Iraq. His essay "Seizing This Teachable Moment"
(distributed by Empower America on August 25, 2003) declared that "children in Iraq are seeing the hand of democracy at work for the first time.
We are rebuilding schools and cities, and restoring justice. The pinnacle of
reconstruction in Iraq will be the establishment of a government of, by, and
for the Iraqi people. But it took our liberation—with military might—to
actually begin this process."

POWER OF EXAMPLE

Senator Jim Jeffords from Vermont gave a strong lesson to Washington and
the country when, revolted by the narrow mindset and policies of the Bush
administration, his independent way of thinking led him to withdrew from
the Republican Party.

Both conservatives and liberals sought models in public life to inspire students to learn and do good things. But did they exist? Richard Nixon and his first vice president were forced out of office and Bill Clinton nearly met the same fate. (Had the press been as candid in the 1960s as in the 1990s, JFK would have been in trouble, too.) Ike and LBJ were decent men but not eloquent like JFK or Clinton. Still, no president butchered the native tongue like Dubya. None had such a sordid record of, at best, semi-legal business transactions. Not for over 100 years had any president done so much for his plutocrat backers at the expense of the public. Even Dubya's well-to-do father had sold his reputation to a cult that claimed Satan had captured America. Senator Jeffords' lesson in integrity did little to alter the main thrust of passionate conservative policies.

BUSINESS ETHICS: "CATS," EMILY DICKINSON OR MACHIAVELLI?

Those who reviewed Dubya's business transactions wondered if he had studied business ethics at Harvard. Still, there were signs that Dubya embodied fundamentals of a liberal education. Receiving an honorary degree from Ohio State in June 2002, the president extolled duty and charity, human fulfillment and patriotism. The address drew on ideas he "derived" from de Tocqueville, Adam Smith, "the world's greatest religions," Aristotle, George Eliot, Emily Dickinson, Wordsworth, Pope John Paul II, Cicero, Lincoln, Jefferson and Washington—this, at least, is what John Bridgeland, director of the U.S.A. Freedom Corps, told the press.

Reporters inferred they had misjudged the president. As Maureen Dowd noted in *The New York Times*, few had ever expected to hear the words "George Eliot" and "George Bush" in the same sentence. Dowd wondered, however, whether the latter George knew that he differed from the former in a fundamental way. Who would have guessed, Dowd wrote, that the man responsible for the immortal locution about immigration— "We need to know who's coming in and why they're not going out"—was inspired by the *Nicomachean Ethics*. Dubya had moved far since the days when his main cultural reference point was *Cats*.

Chapter 7

APPEALS TO FAITH: IN GEORGE WE TRUST?

Passionate conservatives justified much of their agenda by faith rather than by charity. George W. said that he stopped boozing and turned to Jesus in 1985 after meeting the Rev. Billy Graham. The born-again Christian said he would not impose his beliefs on others, even though, as governor, he had proclaimed in 2000 a "Jesus Day" in Texas.

"The powers that be are ordained by God." This statement by St. Paul helped inspire a talk by Supreme Court Justice Antonin Scalia, praised by Bush as a model of judicial greatness. Speaking to the University of Chicago Divinity School in January 2002. Scalia interpreted St. Paul to mean: "The Lord repaid—did justice—through His minister, the state." Scalia said this view represented a consensus "not just of Christian or religious thought, but of secular thought regarding the powers of this state." This consensus, however, "has been upset...by the emergence of democracy." People of faith,

Scalia declared, should not resign themselves to democracy's tendency to obscure the divine authority behind government. They should "combat it as effectively as possible." (*In re* Scalia's duck hunts, see p. 28)

Justice Scalia obviously disagreed with the U.S. Constitution's separation of church and state and with James Madison's warning that religious zeal can lead men "to vex and oppress each other." Scalia instead lined up with other fundamentalists who urge "combat" if their views on law and morality are not embraced by government policy.

The dangers in following religious zealots were underscored in Molière's play, *Tartuffe, or the Impostor*. Cléante is concerned that Orgon, his brother-in-law has been taken in by Tartuffe, an outwardly pious man to whom he gave alms at church. "There are false saints just as there are false heroes," says Cléante. "Real heroes don't make a lot of noise and the truly devout don't make faces." When Orgon wants to sign over all his property to Tartuffe and force his daughter to marry him, Cléante asks: "Can't you tell the difference between hypocrisy and real devotion? Do you honor a mask like a real face? Do you confuse appearance with reality? Esteem a phantom like a real person? Counterfeit with real coin?" Our minds are limited, Cléante observed, and humans often spoil what is most noble.

When Dubya became president, his religious views seemed to shape his policies in many domains—from family planning to school vouchers. It seemed that he wanted to "constitutionalize religion," as the director of the

Texas Civil Rights Project put it. Bush named as U.S. Attorney General the Christian Right favorite John Ashcroft—a man more noted for subverting the law than for enforcing it when he served as Missouri's attorney general. Bush named another strong "pro-life" advocate, Tommy Thompson, to head the Department of Health and Human Services, where he could shape laws on family planning. As governor of Wisconsin, Thompson cut welfare rolls and left more of the state's poorest children without health insurance than before the welfare overhaul.

We cannot read the inner soul of George W. Bush. Is he a God-fearing Christian, as he claims, or a Machiavellian prince who believes in nothing but power and uses religion to advance his own ends?

GOD + GOVERNMENT = ?

His first day on the job, President Dubya proclaimed January 21st a day of prayer and thanksgiving. Pushing to make "faith-based" charities eligible for federal funds, Dubya created a White House Office of Faith-Based and Community Initiatives headed by political scientist John J. DiIulio, Jr. In 1996, then-Senator John Ashcroft inserted into the Welfare Reform Act the principle of "charitable choice," making it easier for religious and charitable groups to compete for federal contracts. In 1997, as governor, George W. sponsored laws allowing churches to provide drug-treatment and other social services without state oversight. Evangelicals rejoiced, but reports of weird cults multiplied. In Corpus Christi, teenagers told police the supervisor of a Christian home had tied and beat them in the name of Christian discipline.

Critics—from Pat Robertson to reform Jewish rabbis—said the "faith" project violated the line between church and state. A different complaint was expressed by DiIulio when he resigned in 2002. He accused Bush of forsaking "compassionate conservatism" for tax cuts. The White House, DiIulio said, was run by a bunch of Mayberry Machiavellis headed by Karl Rove. When DiIulio quickly retracted his assertions as groundless, observers asked if he had wilted under threat.

NOT JUST TAX CUTS BUT
VOUCHERS ALSO CAN WORK WONDERS

Bush sought to appeal to many persuasions. He assured Catholics his faith-based initiative would reduce abortions. The first program George W. sent

to Congress was an educational reform package that included vouchers for private schools. Since the federal government, until then, had provided only 7% of the funding for public schools, such vouchers would introduce a very substantial new role for the federal government. Bush asked a group of Catholic leaders to help him develop a new "PR perspective." Instead of "vouchers," he said, they should be called "opportunity scholarships" or "freedom initiatives."

Playing to the same constituency, Neil Bush let the parochial Nativity School in Cincinnati try out his "Ignite! Learning" teaching toys. But neither Neil nor his other brothers instructed priests how to keep their hands off little boys. Perhaps this was their obeisance to separation of church and state.

SHALL WE SUBSIDIZE JIHAD?

In 2002, Bush's support for faith-based initiatives provided some pupils with vouchers worth just over $2,000—nearly enough to pay tuition at denominational schools (mostly Catholic) but not nearly enough to cover costs at elite academies. Publicly-funded vouchers assisted three out of four pupils attending St. Vitas School, a Catholic institution in Cleveland. These children, all from low-income homes, won the vouchers in a lottery. However, vouchers served only 3,700 of Cleveland's 75,000 pupils not already in private schools.

Passionate conservatives jumped for joy when the U.S Supreme Court ruled 5-4 in June 2002, that school vouchers, as used in Cleveland, did not violate the constitutional mandate to keep church separate from state. But critics complained that government-funded vouchers diverted funds from public education. Also, would public money paid to parochial schools not weaken the separation of church and state? Would reliance on government money not open the door to government regulation of religion?

How would Dubya's patrons react if parents wanted to use vouchers to send their son to a madrassah where he memorized passages extolling *jihad*? If such a school did not exist locally, might the government be obliged to create one so as to put Muslims on an equal footing with other faiths?

AND WHY NOT SCIENTOLOGY?

Since the U.S. government is not allowed to deny access to public accommodation on religious grounds, would Bush favor distributing taxpayer dollars to all faith-based groups—even those that preach racial hatred and religious intolerance? In his election campaign, Dubya had said: "I have a problem with the teachings of Scientology being viewed on the same par as Judaism or Christianity." Would he now want federal funds to go to a drug treatment program run by Scientologists? To an inner-city childcare program run by the Nation of Islam? To stress reduction programs conducted by Wiccans or Satanists? To chanting therapy led by Hare Krishnas? One rabbi asked if Southern Baptists would divert funds to try and convert Jews.

The president tried to skirt such difficulties when he addressed the faith-ful at Milwaukee's Holy Redeemer Institutional Church of God in Christ on July 3, 2002. Dubya said the federal government should not ask, "Does your organization believe in God?" Rather, it should ask: "Does your program work? Are you saving lives?"

SAFETY-LOCKS FOR COLUMBINE

Good values, Dubya maintained, could overcome many problems. In April 2000, the anniversary of the massacre at Columbine High School, Governor Bush went to a school in Temple, Texas, and talked about values—not about gun laws. He said that government should help people understand "that we need to teach our children right from wrong." Unlike Al Gore, presidential candidate George W. opposed gun registration. As governor, Dubya signed a law allowing people to carry concealed weapons. But he also signed a bill increasing penalties for selling guns to juveniles and called for raising the minimum age for handgun possession from 18 to 21. Dubya favored a law requiring instant background checks for gun buyers and said he would sign legislation requiring child-safety locks on handguns.

Fast-forward to election year 2004. President Bush joined the NRA in pressuring Congress to make gun dealers as well as manufacturers immune to civil lawsuits. The White House claimed it wished to prevent "frivolous" litigation. The president urged Republicans to reject two amendments to the immunity bill. One amendment would extend the existing ban on the manufacture and import of specified military assault weapons for ten years. The

second sought to close the "gun show loophole" allowing unlicensed dealers to sell weapons without requesting a government background check. When Democrats won positive votes on these last two amendments on March 2, 2004, the Senate turned down the entire gun law package. Senator McCain and a few other Republicans cheered with Democrats, but House Republicans promised to continue efforts to remove liability from gun makers who, they said, were being sued for making a legal product.

FAITHFUL SEX

Candidate Bush said he did not want to strike from the Republican Party platform its call for a constitutional amendment banning all abortions. But he never promised to ban abortions. Instead, he pledged to "set an ideal" for the nation. "The country I want to live in is a country that respects life of the unborn and the living," he told an interviewer in June 2000. He doubted that abortion would be banned, but urged "we do everything we can to make it more rare."

In 2004, the president called for $1.5 billion in federal funds to promote heterosexual marriage—what White House officials said was a relatively inexpensive but politically expedient initiative that would strengthen the president's standing among conservative Christians upset at the prospect of more homosexual unions. Everything is relative, but special and remedial education were to be boosted by only $1 billion each in fiscal year 2005.

On February 24, 2004, continuing his efforts to limit the powers of the federal government, the president called for a constitutional amendment banning states from recognizing the unions of gay men and women in marriage. He complained that a few judges and local authorities (the Massachusetts Supreme Judicial Court and the mayor of San Francisco) were altering legal and cultural traditions that extended back for centuries and even for millennia.

LIFE, LIBERTY AND ABORTION

The first lady stunned some Bush supporters at an inauguration ceremony in January 2001, when she expressed the view that the Roe v. Wade decision should remain the law of the land—a much stronger endorsement than George W.'s usual statement that voters were not ready to change the 1973 Supreme Court ruling. Dubya had also made it clear that he would like to appoint more justices to the court such as Antonin Scalia and Clarence Thomas who opposed Roe v. Wade.

Laura also endorsed abstinence and abstinence classes. Several days after she spoke, George W. explained his view: "My pro-life position is I believe there's life. It's not necessarily based on religion. I think there's a life there, therefore the notion of life, liberty and pursuit of happiness."—quoted by Joan Ryan in *San Francisco Chronicle*, January 23, 2001.

PUNCHING HOLES IN THE WAR ON CONDOMS

Out of step with many of Dubya's crusades at home and abroad, Secretary of State Colin Powell broke from passionate conservatives on sex as well. He refused to join the war on condoms. Answering a question posed by a young woman in Milan who phoned into MTV on February 15, 2002, Powell urged young people to forget about conservative taboos and protect themselves to prevent AIDS. "In my own judgment, condoms are a way to prevent infection, and therefore...I encourage their use among people who are sexually active."

Liberals applauded but many conservatives complained that Powell's remarks were "reckless" and a "slap in the face" to backers of President Bush.

WASHINGTON LEFT BREASTLESS!

In Fall 2001, Attorney General John Ashcroft objected when a photographer snapped a shot juxtaposing the bare female breast of the Spirit of Justice in a jaunty relationship to the AG's mouth. A few months later, in January 2002, Justice Department officials curtained off the offending body parts with a blue fabric costing more than $8,650. "A blue burka for Justice?" asked Maureen Dowd in *The New York Times*. The ensuing brouhaha, known as "Drapegate," according to *The Columbus Dispatch*, "leaves Washington

breastless." "At least he didn't blow them up," said the *Houston Chronicle*," comparing Ashcroft favorably with the Taliban.

Denial spin began immediately. Ashcroft's spokeswoman, Barbara Comstock, assured the public in late January 2002, that the AG had nothing to do with the cover-up. "He spends his time dealing with threat assessments and more important business." Purchasing the drapery, she noted, was cheaper than renting one for each occasion the AG met the press.

FAITH-CONSTRAINED SCIENCE?

The production of the first cloned human embryo, announced by Korean scientists in February 2004, underscored the price the U.S. might pay for its restraints on research using embryonic stem cells. In August 2001, the White House decided to allow research using only human embryonic cells created before that date. This limitation reflected the influence of the anti-abortion lobby, convinced that dissecting a blastocyst amounts to murder, and the view of the chairman of the President's Council on Bioethics that science should not be allowed into life's central mysteries. Many U.S. scientists complained that they were constrained from advancing into realms that could regenerate the body's tissues.

It was not just religious agendas which constrained American science under George W. Bush. On February 18, 2004, more than 60 leading scientists—including Nobel Laureates, leading medical experts, former federal agency directors and university chairs and presidents—issued a statement calling for regulatory and legislative action to restore scientific integrity to federal policymaking. The report charged that the Bush administration suppressed and distorted scientific analysis from federal agencies and took actions that were harmful to the quality of scientific advisory panels. "Whether the issue is lead paint, clean air or climate change, this behavior has serious consequences for all Americans," said Dr. Kurt Gottfried, professor emeritus of physics at Cornell University and Chairman of the Union of Concerned Scientists. The Union's report, titled *Scientific Integrity in Policymaking:*

An Investigation into the Bush Administration's Misuse of Science, began by quoting President Bush's father, who declared in 1990 that "science...relies on freedom of inquiry...and objectivity." But, said Russell Train, head of the EPA under Nixon and Ford, the George W. Bush administration "obstructed that freedom and distorted that objectivity in ways...unheard of in any previous administration." "In case after case, scientific input to policymaking is being censored and distorted"—with "serious consequences for public health," said Dr. Neal Lane, a former director of the National Science Foundation and a former presidential science adviser. The scientists demanded a halt to the "distortion of scientific knowledge for partisan political ends." They called for Congressional oversight hearings, guaranteed public access to government scientific studies and other measures to prevent such abuses in the future. Other studies warned that the United States was losing its preeminence in science and technology as Americans focused on practical affairs and fewer foreign brains opted to study and work in the U.S.

SOME CLONES SUPERIOR TO OTHERS?

"It would be a mistake for the United States Senate to allow any kind of human cloning to come out of that chamber."—GWB quoted in *The Times* (London), April 18, 2002.

Despite the Bush administration's reservations about stem cell research, some observers wondered if Republicans would not be pleased to generate replicas of such GOP greats as Richard Nixon, Ronald Reagan and perhaps even George the Elder and George the Younger.

WHEN ARE EXECUTIONS JUST? DOES IT MATTER?

Machiavelli told the prince not to worry whether capital punishment was just. But in 2001, Supreme Court Justice Sandra Day O'Connor admitted to "serious questions" about whether the penalty was being fairly administered. Often casting the swing vote in the Supreme Court, she had for years staunchly supported the death penalty. In 2001, however, she noted that in the last three decades, 90 inmates condemned had been found innocent and set free. In Texas, said O'Connor, defendants with court-appointed lawyers were much more likely to receive the death penalty than those who hired their own lawyers. As she spoke, some 3,711 persons sat on death rows throughout the country.

Winds of change: In 2002, the Supreme Court in Atkins v. Virginia banned execution of the mentally retarded, and in Ring v. Arizona it overturned up to 168 death sentences in states where juries have been excluded from capital sentencing decisions. The New York City Council called for a moratorium on the death penalty. The governor of Illinois commuted all death sentences. All these do-gooders, according to Machiavelli, were misguided.

APOCALYPSE NOW (BUT DONATIONS WELCOME ANYWAY)

Just two days after 9/11, the Rev. Jerry Falwell explained to a large audience what caused the mayhem. Speaking on Rev. Pat Robertson's TV show, Falwell blamed America's misfortunes on "throwing God out of the public square, out of the schools.... And when we destroy 40 million little innocent babies, we make God mad. [The] pagans, and the abortionists, and the feminists, and the gays and lesbians who are actively trying to make that an alternative lifestyle, the ACLU, People for the American Way—all of them who have tried to secularize America—I point the finger in their face and say, 'You helped this happen.'"

Having ignited a flack storm, Falwell one day later claimed that his comments were made during "a long theological discussion" and had been "taken out of context." His son, the Rev. Jonathan Falwell, added that "Satan has launched a hail of fiery darts at Dad" and that "liberals, and especially gay activists, have launched a vicious smear campaign to discredit him." Jonathan suggested that supporters ease Dad's "personal hurt" by sending "a special Vote of Confidence gift" of $50 or $100!

Is it possible that such fanatics, as money-grubbing as they are narrow-minded, could influence what the Bush White House does? Born-again Bush, like Falwell, sees the United States as "good" in a war against "evil

ones" and "evil doers." Both men support the American Christian and Jewish Zionists who back Prime Minister Sharon's efforts to reestablish the borders of ancient Israel. Bush has tempered his language about a crusade against Islamic terrorists, but Falwell has not. His weekly ministry Web site pillories Mohammed "the terrorist" for backing *jihad* and polygamy.

One hopes that Dubya did not wish to trigger an apocalypse when he attacked Iraq, but Falwell in 2002 preached that America must fight Iraq

to catalyze the second coming of Christ and the end of the world. While Falwell backs Israel just now, he teaches that only those Jews and non-Jews (Muslims, Catholics, Buddhists, etc.) who convert to Evangelical Christianity will be saved. A battle fought in Armageddon (in northern Israel) will put Jerry Falwell at the right hand of God (cbsnews.com October 6, 2002 and June 9, 2003).

All parties might benefit from St. Augustine's admonition: "Do not try to fight evil as if it arises from outside yourself." Meanwhile, the president energized many passionate conservative votes by calling for a constitutional amendment to ban gay marriage, a practice fomented by some judges and city officials in the putative Sodom and Gomorra of modern America, Boston and San Francisco.

"I have a different vision of leadership. A leadership is someone who brings people together."

George W. Bush
August 18, 2000

Chapter 8

US AND THEM: HOW TO LOSE
FRIENDS AND INSPIRE ENEMIES

When representatives of the thirteen United States of America decided in July, 1776, to claim a "separate and equal station" among the powers of the earth, they stated that "a decent respect for the opinions of mankind" led them to "declare the causes which impel them to the separation." The U.S. Constitution, drawn up eleven years later, established that "all treaties made, or which shall be made, under the authority of the United States, shall be the supreme law of the land," along with the U.S. Constitution and all laws made pursuant to it.

Unlike America's Founding Fathers, the Bush team showed almost no "respect for the opinions of mankind"—or for treaties and other forms of international law. Indeed, as we see throughout this book, Dubya and his people also showed little respect for the U.S. Constitution and its Bill of Rights. As president, Dubya trashed his campaign principle that the U.S. should act with "humility" on the world scene.

At the beginning of the 21st century, the U.S. was an unrivaled super-power presiding over a *pax Americana*. A true conservative would try to pro-long and enhance the unipolar stability that took shape in the 1990s. A wise superpower would avoid needless offense to others' sensitivities. It would twist arms only if hard pressed on vital issues. A "decent respect for the opinions of mankind" would make it easier to reap influence from power.

From the day George W. Bush entered the White House, however, the Bush team seemed almost determined to alienate America's traditional friends and antagonize others so they become foes rather than partners. Dubya and his people ignored understandings built up among many countries over many years and demanded that others bow to whatever new rules were invented in Washington. Instead of bolstering American influence, Dubya's policies provoked the emergence of hostile coalitions eager to defy Washington and knock America from its pedestal.

A skilled diplomat seldom says "No." He or she says "maybe" or "let's try another approach." Even Vladimir Lenin instructed Soviet diplomats in 1922 to "avoid biting words." Time after time, however, the Bush White House brusquely said "no" to deals that had been carefully negotiated by previous U.S. presidents with other governments. Sometimes the Bush White House promised to come up with an alternative but it seldom did so.

Revulsion against internationalism was fueled in part by American exceptionalism—the belief that the U.S. is God's elected instrument to be the boss of the humanity and teach it virtue. But private greed also played a role. Thus, in 2001, the Bush administration pulled away from a multinational accord to clamp down on tax havens. The White House piously affirmed that everyone should pay taxes, but it opposed unnecessary regulations! A set of big businesses and major contributors to Republican causes applauded. In this same spirit, Washington joined Tokyo in undermining a pact endorsed by some 150 countries to ban cigarette advertising—a "violation of free speech guarantees sacred to Americans," the U.S. delegation protested, as American tobacco growers Jim Beamed.

WHO OR WHAT CAN REPLACE THE EVIL EMPIRE?

Dubya did not participate in the Cold War unless to look for women on chilly nights in Beijing when Dad was U.S. Ambassador to China. Dubya's chief deputies, however, had been deeply involved: Vice President Dick Cheney

and Pentagon chief Donald Rumsfeld had each headed the Pentagon before the Clinton era. Secretary of State Colin Powell had been chairman of the Joint Chiefs of Staff. National Security Advisor Condoleezza Rice had served on the National Security Council under George the Elder. When Dubya's top men and woman arrived back in Washington in 2001, they scanned the horizon for a unifying adversary to replace the USSR, which had imploded in 1991. Initially, they seized on China as the lead candidate. After 9/11, however, they targeted al Qaeda and the Taliban. In 2002, after the U.S. took Kabul, the U.S. president designated an "axis of evil"—Iraq, North Korea, and Iran—against which the U.S. would struggle. Lesser places of dishonor in a rogue's gallery were retained by Fidel Castro, Muammar Al-Qaddafi, and Yasser Arafat. In 2002, Bush called for the creation of a Palestinian state but, as a precondition, stipulated that Arafat had to go.

Election year 2004 saw the president demonstrate for Cubans in Florida his commitment to "bring democracy to Cuba" by broadcasting Radio and TV Marti signals from a plane flying around the island, thus by-passing Fidel's jamming devices. Qaddafi buckled in 2004 but Fidel did not, while Arafat endured under siege.

"I BELIEVE WHAT I BELIEVE IS RIGHT"

On his first visit to Europe as U.S. president, George W. met with European Union leaders in Gothenburg, Sweden. He faced a set of allies deeply opposed to what they saw as American unilateralism. Before Bush's arrival French President Jacques Chirac and German Chancellor Gerhard Schroeder prepared a joint statement critical of Bush policies. Many Europeans had long opposed American use of the death penalty. Now they met a man who, when he served as governor of Texas, seemed to view executions as a sign of public virtue. Having become U.S. president, Bush denounced the Kyoto protocol on global warming—seen by many Europeans as crucial to saving the planet. And he declared American determination to build anti-missile defenses forbidden by the 1972 treaty on ballistic missile defense—a treaty widely regarded as a foundation for international security.

Later, in Rome, Bush explained: "I know what I believe. I will continue to articulate what I believe and what I believe—I believe what I believe is right." (Reuters, July 23, 2001).

BARE CONFRONTATIONS IN THE OLD WORLD

In Sweden, the European Union leaders expressed their opposition to President Bush with words, but some street demonstrators mooned for naked honesty. Some threw stones at mounted Swedish police wearing riot gear, while others dropped their pants.

National Security Advisor Condoleezza Rice may have tried to alleviate the president's concerns (if he had any). Helping pave the way for Bush (and herself) into the White House, she had briefed Dubya on foreign affairs in 2000—sometimes as she worked out on a treadmill and he on a glider in Crawford. Even though she was known as a hardline realist, "Condi" may have resisted any tit-for-tat response to the demonstrators in Sweden.

Despite disagreements, Bush and the Europeans agreed to work together in combating AIDS and other communicable diseases, especially in Africa. As Dubya put it to the press corps on June 14, 2001: "We spent a lot of time talking about Africa, as we should. Africa is a nation [*sic*] that suffers from incredible disease [*sic*]." In 2003, Bush visited five African countries and promised a huge infusion of dollars for AIDS research and treatment, but Congress dragged its feet while the White House sermoned for sexual abstinence.

ONE FIGUREHEAD TO ANOTHER

Greeted by a royal guard of honor, President George W. Bush dropped in on the Queen at Buckingham Palace on July 19, 2001. Joined by Laura Bush and the Duke of Edinburgh, the two heads of state took lunch together. Hav-

ing renounced liquor after previous mishaps, George W. kept to his teetotal
regime. Still, Dubya and the Queen had something in common: Based on
how the Bush dynasty's connections helped George W. come to power, he,
too, could be seen as a figurehead.

BLOWBACK

Angered by Bush's unilateralism, Europeans joined with China and some
third world countries to exclude the U.S. from the United Nations Human
Rights Commission in 2001.

"An 800-pound gorilla just doesn't like anything to restrict its freedom
of action" is how Harvard professor Stephen Walt described Washington's
response to the International Criminal Court (ICC), set up by 74 countries
in June 2002. The gorilla responded in unprecedented ways. The Bush team
claimed to "un-sign" the court's basic statute signed a few years earlier by
the Clinton administration. Congress considered a law claiming a U.S. right
to use "all means necessary" to rescue any Americans detained by the court.
Washington announced it would block all UN peacekeeping missions unless
Americans were exempted from ICC jurisdiction. Following through on that
threat, the U.S. cast America's 75th veto at the Security Council to block
extension of two UN missions in Bosnia.

Washington's refusal to approve UN peacekeeping actions without an
exclusion for U.S. forces from ICC jurisdiction meant that all peacekeeping
operations might be terminated one by one as they came up for renewal.

PASSIONATE CONSERVATISM TWISTS THE KNIFE

On his first working day as president, Bush halted federal funding of international family planning programs that provided abortion services or abortion counseling, a ban imposed by Ronald Reagan in 1984 but later reversed by Bill Clinton.

As America attacked the Taliban, Laura Bush lamented the conditions endured by Afghan women. In October 2001, the U.S. sent $600,000 to the UN Fund for Population to provide emergency birthing kits and sanitary supplies to Afghan refugees in Iran, Pakistan, Uzbekistan and Tajikistan. In 2002, the U.S. foreign aid bill included $34 million for the UN Fund. But then the pro-life Population Research Institute accused the UN agency of supporting forced abortions and sterilization in China. When Rep. Chris Smith (R-N.J.) asked the president to withhold the money, he did so. In July 2002, the United States cut off its $34 million contribution to the UN Fund for Population—over the objections of Secretary of State Colin Powell and moderate Republicans.

Calling the U.S. action "irresponsible and counter-productive," the European Union stepped in and replaced the $34 million that Washington withheld. The EU estimated that 80,000 women were dying every year from unsafe abortions. Official Washington and Europe continued to ignore ghastly civil carnage in the Sudan and in west Africa—even in Liberia, settled by American blacks. Had somebody struck oil, as in Nigeria, the West may have shown more concern.

NUANCED OPTIONS

UK Prime Minister Tony Blair stood by the White House no matter what—almost. On Iraq, however, Blair tried for a while to keep his distance from U.S. determination to oust Saddam Hussein by force. When Dubya hosted Tony at the Prairie Chapel ranch in Texas in April 2002, the U.S. leader used gung-ho language calling for action against Saddam. Bush told the press: "Look, my job isn't to try to nuance; my job is to tell people what I think." The British PM, however, assured worriers there would be no "precipitate" action against Iraq. Insiders said that Dubya believed Tony would join him when the time came. Bush wanted to finish the job his father cut short in 1991, while Blair responded to anxieties within his own Labour Party and on the Continent.

Bush praised Blair because "this Prime Minister...does not need a focus group to convince him of the difference between right and wrong." Blair allowed that "all the options are open."

Mr. Blair's policy choices, it emerged, had included bugging the offices of UN Secretary-General Kofi Annan to get information on the attitudes of other UN Security Council members on attacking Iraq. Political realists said this was business as usual in world politics. But Blair's credibility sank another notch for those hoping he would pull Washington to observe higher standards of international law.

BRITAIN'S MOST UNPOPULAR VISITOR SINCE 1066

In November 2003, after UK forces joined the U.S. in attacking Iraq and removing Saddam Hussein's regime in March-April, Dubya and Laura made an official state visit to the UK. The trip was planned before the Iraq war and followed Blair's visit to the U.S. in July 2003, when he got a warm reception addressing both houses of Congress. So worried was the U.S. Secret Service that its agents (some 250 strong) wanted to shut down central London and close sections of the Underground for three days. It wanted to strengthen the walls and windows of Buckingham Palace. It installed so much electronics there that the Queen's TV reception suffered. But 43% of the British public welcomed the Bushes, and only 36% opposed the visit. Still, tens of thousands protested, tearing down a replica statue of Dubya in Trafalgar Square. Some protestors called Bush the "most unpopular visitor since William the Conqueror" in 1066. To preclude heckling like that which greeted Bush when he spoke to the Australian parliament in October 2003, the president did not address the UK parliament. Instead, he spoke with a small group of academics and visited a tavern in Blair's home constituency.

HOW THE U.S. BECAME ITS OWN WORST ENEMY

While U.S.-UK ties remained fairly strong, the excesses of Bush's unilateralism divided the West and reduced its ability to function as a united force for good on the world scene. The U.S. under Bush, some said, had become its own worst enemy.

The UK kept its own currency, sterling, and did not for the present join the euro. But some Americans, as well as many Europeans, found life simpler when they did not have to change currency when changing frontiers. Americans especially liked the euro when it was valued at less than the dollar in 2001. Thanks to Bushonomics and the burgeoning U.S. federal deficit, however, the dollar fell below the euro in 2002 and kept sliding through 2003. The dollar's fall boosted U.S. exports but threatened to induce foreign investors to withdraw their investments from U.S. stocks and government bonds.

BUSH-STYLE HUMILITY ON THE WORLD SCENE

Seeing the world as us versus them, the Bush team continued to alienate friends and inspire enemies. Unlike Bush the Elder, the 43rd president did not seek collective security but relied on unilateral force, supplemented by help from the UK and some lesser powers anxious for U.S. approval and side-payments. The approach led Americans into a blind alley in post-Saddam Iraq, where U.S. troops were too few, too hated and sometimes too uninformed about local ways to provide security for themselves or for Iraqis. The Bush team took a deep breath and asked other countries to send troops and police to help stabilize Iraq. Some did—Poland, Spain, Italy, plus some smaller allies such as Estonia. But help from India and many other states was limited by Washington's insistence on keeping crucial decision making under its control. (More details in chapter 14.)

Jimmy Carter observed that "unilateral acts and assertions increasingly isolate the United States from the very nations needed to join in combating terrorism." These acts included "peremptory rejections of nuclear arms agreements, the biological weapons convention, environmental protection, anti-torture proposals and punishment of war criminals...sometimes combined with economic threats against those who might disagree with us."

Despite receiving a cold shoulder from Washington, the UN tried to play a constructive role in rebuilding Iraq. In August 2003, however, terrorists bombed UN headquarters in Baghdad, killing the top UN diplomat and 21 others.

Chapter 9

MAKING THE WORLD SAFE FOR AMERICANS: PREEMPT!

When the 21st century began, threats to the U.S. could be graded: A-type threats came from Russia and China—both armed with nuclear-tipped missiles. Grade B threats came from Iraq and North Korea—each seeking weapons of mass destruction. C-type threats arose from the Balkans, where local conflict could spread and drag in NATO and perhaps Russia. The Arab-Israeli confrontation was also grade C but could escalate to B or A. Ethnic conflicts in Africa and South Asia were grade D—often horrible but remote from U.S. interests.

After September 11, 2001, the picture seemed more complex. Americans now realized that A-type threats could arise from "asymmetrical" warfare waged by individuals, groups or countries able to turn modern technology against the United States. On September 11, terrorists used civilian airliners; next time they might exploit nuclear, biological or chemical weapons. Americans could not count on "deterrence" (terrorization) to restrain those ready to die for their goals.

Faced with threats from within and without, the U.S. needs "hard power" to deter, command or coerce others; "soft power" to enlist allies and dissuade potential foes; and "conversion power"—the leadership and other qualities needed to utilize these assets effectively. Wise leadership is needed to allocate resources to deal with threats today and tomorrow, while nurturing assets needed for the long run—a strong economy, social cohesion, education and public health.

Against the USSR, the United States relied on deterrence. After the Soviet demise in 1991, the Pentagon sought an ability to fight and win two regional wars simultaneously, while conducting a major peacekeeping or humanitarian mission (as in Haiti). When Dubya entered the White House, he downplayed deterrence and focused on defense—active defense to destroy incoming missiles. China replaced Russia as the major rival.

The terrorist actions on September 11, 2001, produced another change. Focused on fighting terror, Bush asked China and Russia to help this cause. Before 9/11, Bush wanted to build a Fortress America. Now he resolved to seek out and destroy enemy forces before they could hit American targets, even while mobilizing all agencies to fight and neutralize hostile agents within the U.S.

The U.S. "intelligence community" spent about $30 billion a year before 9/11—about one-tenth as much as the entire Defense Department. The lion's share went for spy satellites and eavesdropping hardware, with relatively few resources for "humint"—spies on the ground, trained in foreign tongues and cultures—and, most crucially, analysis to "connect the dots". After 9/11, the Bush team resolved to improve America's "information operations." The 2002 *Nuclear Posture Review* called for exploiting enemy computer networks and integrating cyber-warfare into the overall nuclear war database to achieve more effective targeting and combat-assessment. The review said nothing about any need to have dependable agents able to talk with people in Cairo or Tunis, Shanghai or Guangzhou, but the CIA placed more ads (for example, in *The Economist*) for potential James Bonds.

Environmental security was also at risk from climate change and pollution. By 2002, three years of drought had knocked Kansas from the pedestal of wheat-producing states. Homes in Alaska were sinking as their foundations melted. Forest fires in Quebec covered New York and Pennsylvania with a thick haze. The Maldives and other island nations were slipping beneath the waves. Would this happen soon to Florida?

The Bush team distorted security priorities. It cut taxes—mainly for a wealthy few—returning the country to deficit spending. It eroded confidence in the U.S. economy, frightening both American and foreign investors. To deal with mounting energy needs it promoted oil exploration, not only in environmentally fragile parts of the U.S., but also in politically explosive regions abroad such as the Caspian Sea. It virtually ignored energy conservation and alternatives to oil-gas-coal dependency.

Before and after September 11, the Bush Administration worked to scuttle the antiballistic missile (ABM) treaty that President Richard Nixon signed with the Soviet Union in 1972, and to replace it with a national missile defense. If the new defenses worked at all, they might be most useful against a limited attack by North Korea. The Clinton administration had negotiated a "Framework Agreement" in 1994 to halt North Korea's production of fissionable materials. Later, in 2000, it nearly concluded a deal with Pyongyang to limit North Korea's manufacture, testing and export of missiles. But, in 2001, Dubya permitted these negotiations to lapse, explaining that the North Koreans could not be trusted. In so doing, the president helped destroy one of the greatest arms control achievements of the 1990s—an arrangement to de-fang North Korea's nuclear capability in exchange for a few

billion dollars of fuel oil and nuclear power equipment provided by Japan, South Korea and the United States.[1]

Instead of utilizing the United Nations and international law as potential partners in forging a new world order, the Bush team treated them with scorn. This was penny-wise and pound-foolish many times over. If the UN did the job, the United States might have to pay one-fourth the cost (less than the U.S. share of world GDP). If Americans did the same job by themselves, they would foot the entire bill.

WHAT YOU DON'T KNOW CAN HURT SOMEBODY ELSE

Except for Colin Powell, most top policymakers in Dubya's Washington had no personal experience with military life. They had not experienced a weapon malfunction; a misguided bomb; the death or wounds of a comrade. Few top policymakers had lived abroad. Fewer still had lived among the peoples who generated sons and daughters determined to destroy America. Like Robert Strange McNamara, Pentagon chief as Americans marched into Vietnam, Bush and most of his national security apparatus knew war only as a set of abstractions. Yes, Dubya's father was a World War II hero who later lived in China. But such experiences were rare among those politicians who faced—but avoided—military duty in the 1960s and 1970s—Senators John McCain and John F. Kerry being notable exceptions.

In his booklet *On Perpetual Peace* Immanuel Kant predicted that democracies, unlike kings, would be loath to initiate optional wars because voters knew their own lives would be at risk. Would this theory apply to a policymaking elite shielded from physical danger while commanding a professional force, whose movements Congress left up to the president?

IN BED WITH A COMPLEX

As he left the White House in 1961, Dwight Eisenhower warned that the U.S. risked domination by its own military-industrial complex—a cabal of back-scratching buddies who enriched each other at the public's expense. The complex welcomed President Ronald Reagan's Strategic Defense Initiative, launched in 1983, to erect an astrodome shield against intercontinental ballistic missiles (ICBMs). Each year thereafter, the Pentagon spent more than $3 billion on ABM research and testing—nearly $100 billion by 2000. The studies showed that a defensive missile might hit an incoming warhead, but no way was found to discriminate between a real warhead and a decoy. Nonetheless Boeing, Lockheed, Raytheon and other units of the military-industrial complex enjoyed juicy contracts from what some security experts termed "Star Wars madness."

Polls conducted by Boston University students from 1980 through 2003 showed that more than 90% of Americans believed the U.S. already had an ABM system capable of shooting down a large fraction of attacking ICBMs. Could a citizenry so ill-informed about national security give sound guidance to its representatives in Washington?

CAN ANTIMISSILE MISSILES STOP SUITCASE BOMBS?

It was impossible to defend against Russian or Chinese ICBMs because their offensive weapons could readily overwhelm any ABM defense. Against smaller, less sophisticated "rogue states," an ABM defense might be unnecessary. North Korea might still be dissuaded from perfecting an ICBM

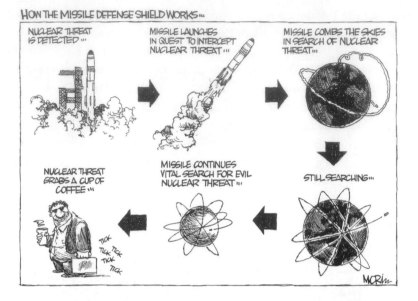

delivery system. Iran and Iraq lagged still further. If any rogue state seemed to be developing a workable ICBM, America could destroy it on the ground.

The Maginot Line gave France a false sense of security in the 1930s. When Hitler attacked, German forces went around the French defenses. An ingenious attacker might find a way to pierce or outflank the best defenses. An elaborate ABM network would not have stopped the 9/11 skyjackings. The CIA warned that rogue states and terrorist groups could find cheaper,

easier and more dependable ways to strike the U.S. than by attempting to obtain ICBMs. Nukes or other weapons of mass destruction could arrive in trucks, by ship, small planes and even in suitcases. Cruise missiles fired from a ship or other platform would fly under ABM radar. But Dubya and Defense Secretary Rumsfeld ordered their ABM makers to "carry on, carry on."

HOW TO REBUILD THE BEIJING-MOSCOW AXIS

Critics said the tests were rigged, but Dubya and Rumsfeld were pleased when on several occasions a defensive missile fired from a Pacific island intercepted and destroyed the simulated warhead on an ICBM fired from California. The White House asserted the tests showed that ABM defense was feasible.

But as U.S. engineers opened the ground in Alaska for ABM launchers, China and Russia drew closer together. Neither wanted its deterrents to be downgraded. In 2001, China had about twenty missiles that could reach the U.S., but threatened to build more and better weapons to penetrate any defense. If the U.S. built an ABM, Russia warned it would not ratify the Strategic Arms Reduction Treaty ("START 2") signed by George Bush the Elder and Mikhail Gorbachev. Not only did that treaty compel each side to cut its missile forces by a large fraction, it also forbade deployment of multiple warheads on each missile. Freed from that restraint, Russia could put many warheads on its newest missiles—a defense nightmare for America.

Bush pushed the world's largest countries—in population and in territory—to realign against the U.S. Would that make Americans more secure?

CONSERVATIVES VS. THE LAW

In December 2001, President Bush said the U.S. would withdraw from the 1972 ABM treaty in six months. What would replace it? An unproven defense system that, at best, might make an enemy wonder if some of its missiles might not be deflected. Instead of consulting NATO partners, the Bush administration informed them to expect changes in U.S. policy. Not only Russia and China, but America's NATO allies also protested.

In June 2002, just before the abrogation would become effective, Dennis J. Kucinich (D-Ohio) and 32 other members of the House of Representatives filed suit against Bush, saying his action was unconstitutional. Citing Thomas Jefferson and over 50 precedents, the plaintiffs argued that since a treaty is part of the "supreme law of the land," and must be made with the approval of Congress, the president alone cannot unmake a treaty. The U.S. District Court, however, upheld the executive branch.

Immanuel Kant was wrong about democratic restraint on military activity. Not only did the president not consult with Congress but the Pentagon even refused to tell Congress how the ABM project was proceeding or what it might cost. It exempted missile defense projects from the reporting requirements normally applied to major acquisition projects.

HOW TO SHOOT YOURSELF IN THE FOOT IN OUTER SPACE

The U.S. had more and better space technology than any other country. Rumsfeld embraced the high-tech "Revolution in Military Affairs." So why not deploy U.S. forces in outer space before any antagonist gained a foothold there? If Washington gave the go-ahead, could not Americans gain a near monopoly in space weapons to zap earthly targets as well as those in the atmosphere and outer space?

Critics pointed out that the U.S. was bound by treaties not to claim the moon or any planet as its territory or to deploy any weapon of mass destruction in outer space. They asked if it could be moral to militarize still more of the global commons. Would it even be in America's interest to tempt other states to deploy their own weapons against U.S. satellites? No country depended more on outer space for communications and reconnaissance than the U.S. How could America gain from an arms race in space? In 2002, Representative Kucinich introduced bills to ban the "weaponization of space" and to create a U.S. Department of Peace, but Washington's momentum was in the opposite direction.

On January 14, 2004, the president promised voters the moon and Mars to boot. By 2020, the U.S. would establish an "extended human presence" on the moon at practically no cost over the present NASA budget for the next five years, with manned trips to Mars to follow. Dubya's main target was probably the November 2004, election, but a base on the moon would also give America military "high ground." Pressed to save money for pie in the sky, NASA decided not to keep the Hubble telescope (one of the most valuable scientific enterprises in outer space) in operation. In 1989, George I had promised manned exploration of Mars by 2019, but that plan fizzled when cost estimates hit $400 billion.

DEPARTMENTS OF EVASION

In April 2001, a Peruvian Air Force jet shot down a Cessna hydroplane carrying American missionaries, believing them to be cocaine smugglers, even though the Cessna was one of five civilian craft regularly flying from Iquitos. The Peruvians machine-gunned the plane after it crashed in the Amazon river, killing a mother and her baby, and wounding the pilot. Villagers in canoes then rescued the pilot and two other survivors.

CIA observers flying nearby in a Citation-5 leased from the Pentagon had monitored the Peruvian jet. "Our role was to simply pass on information," said President Bush. "Our government is involved with helping our friends in South America identify airplanes that might be carrying illegal drugs." The U.S. embassy in Lima explained that U.S. government tracking aircraft "are unarmed and do not participate in any way in shooting down suspect planes."

Here was another case where the Americans preferred a military solution, on foreign territory, to dealing with their own problems. The CIA collaborated with Peru under a $1.3 billion "Plan Columbia" aimed at staunching drug supplies from Latin America. Would not victory in the "war on drugs" require reducing—or ignoring—demand within the U.S.?

In 2003, Colombian drug lords shot down and killed some American mercenaries in the war on drugs and kept others hostage. In 2004, relatives complained that Washington ignored Americans hired to fight unofficially in distant jungles.

AGAINST BALKANIZATION

The Bush White House complained that U.S. troops were losing their fighting edge by serving with peacekeepers in Bosnia and Kosovo. From a total of 1,365,800 men and women in the U.S. Armed Forces (backed by 1,181,700 ready reserves and nearly one million civilians), just over 10,000 were serving in the Balkans and elsewhere on peacekeeping missions in 2001—before 9/11. In East Timor there were two U.S. observers. The work they did in Bosnia and Kosovo required diplomacy as well as military alertness. It underscored the vital link between military strength and policy objectives. Peacekeepers were serving U.S. objectives and broadening their own skills, some of which came in handy later on in Afghanistan and Iraq.

Dubya disparaged "nation-building" before he took office, but much that NATO troops did in the Balkans was essential for peace in the region. A few hundred U.S. troops stationed in Macedonia since the 1990s helped prevent conflicts within Serbia from overflowing into Macedonia. Later, when ethnic Albanians within Macedonia fought for autonomy against the Slavic majority in Macedonia, U.S. and other NATO forces helped make peace between the two sides. In Macedonia the ethnic balance was the opposite from Kosovo, where an Albanian-speaking majority (mostly Muslim) faced a Slavic-speaking, Christian minority. In Macedonia, Kosovo and Bosnia, NATO tried to balance the needs of diverse ethnic groups.

LONG AFTER THE
SHOOTING SUBSIDES

While big bucks went to preparing for new wars, veterans of past wars lived with a wide range of war-induced ailments. Former Senators Bob Dole and Dan Inoue managed to cope with severe wounds received during World War II, but many other vets were less successful. Many Korean vets felt forgotten. One ex-Marine compensated with a bumper sticker: "The Chosin Few" (named for the Chosin Reservoir," where Marines executed one of the greatest fighting retreats in modern history). Vietnam vets endured a variety of ills—perhaps including the effects of Agent Orange. Authorities said as many as 15% of the 700,000 Americans who served in the Persian Gulf might bear problems linked to the 1991 conflict—memory loss, numbness in limbs, sleep disturbance, menstrual disorders and gastrointestinal problems. A University of Texas study found evidence of brain damage in soldiers complaining of Gulf War illness symptoms. Some vets of the Kosovo campaign said they suffered from exposure to depleted uranium weapons. The budget for the U.S. Department of Veterans Affairs for 2003 totaled $58 billion—nearly half of it for medical care. Still, many vets felt their needs were unmet.

The White House labored to minimize public attention on the thousands of American veterans returned from Iraq minus a leg or an arm, or with other wounds. It permitted few pictures of the 500 or so coffins de-planed from Iraq in 2003, usually at night.

HOW NUKES SMALL AND LARGE
CAN SERVE U.S. OBJECTIVES

The Bush team delivered its *Nuclear Posture Review* to Congress on January 8, 2002. Though classified, it soon leaked. The *NPR* said the Pentagon was no longer to regard nuclear weapons as a last resort to be used when survival hung in the balance. Instead, U.S. strategists would plan for contingencies in which America might use nuclear weapons against seven or more adversaries—Iraq, Iran, North Korea (the "axis of evil" trio) plus Libya, Syria, Russia and China (perhaps in a showdown over Taiwan). Nukes might be used to retaliate against chemical or biological weapons attacks, to hit targets able to withstand nonnuclear attack, or to deal with "surprising military developments." Smaller nukes might be used to bust bunkers such as al Qaeda's mountain headquarters. America would also develop "new nonnuclear strategic capabilities" to destroy enemy stores of chemical and biological materials.

The Bush *NPR* looked naïve. It aspired to minimize "collateral damage" while using nuclear weapons against hard targets! It counted on cruise missiles and drones to strike and destroy enemy forces without much need to fight them on the ground, occupy defeated lands, replace regimes or rebuild defeated countries—aseptic war, trouble-free and virtually painless for Americans.

NEW MEDICINE FROM
A STRANGE DOCTOR

National Security Advisor Condoleezza Rice did not look like Dr. Strangelove but she could think and talk like him. In 2002, she rationalized the plans of the Bush Administration to attack and destroy foreign foes before they could attack the U.S. In June 2002, she noted that President John F. Kennedy had "thought about a lot of possibilities," including a pre-emptive strike against Soviet missiles in Cuba. Responding to Dr. Rice, Kennedy's special counsel Ted Sorensen acknowledged that JFK had "thought about" a pre-emptive strike. But, Sorensen went on, Kennedy then rejected this option. He did not want to kill civilians without warning, risk a wider war and lose the moral high ground. "The trouble with a pre-emptive strike doctrine," Sorensen said, "is that it pre-empts the president's own choices." For details, see *The New York Times*, June 17 and July 1, 2002.

Yes, Israel succeeded in destroying Iraq's "Osiraq" nuclear plant from the air in 1981, but a "surgical" air strike without huge collateral damage is very difficult to achieve. Blowing up a reactor or stores of biological or chemical weapons could spread poisons far and wide.

WHO NEEDS CONGRESS IF WE
HAVE A COMMANDER-IN-CHIEF?

President George W. demanded the removal of Saddam Hussein's regime in Iraq. How to effect such a "regime change"? In 2002, top U.S. planners rejected an Afghanistan-style campaign built around air strikes and the use of special operation forces in tandem with Iraqi opposition groups. A Pentagon planning document leaked to the press in July 2002, suggested that the military brass was considering a large-scale air and ground assault involving as many as 250,000 troops.

Could American democracy be reconciled with an offensive war? Only the U.S. Congress may declare war or authorize the funds for large military campaigns. Yes, the president is commander-in-chief. And, after 9/11, Congress gave him a broad mandate to repulse terrorists. But did this mandate include a major attack on a sovereign state? Many Congressional leaders of both parties agreed that Saddam should go. But when would they fulfill their duty to debate whether and how to go to war?

WORST CASE WORRIES

Within weeks of 9/11, the brains behind *MacGyver, Die Hard, Delta Force One, Missing in Action, Fight Club* and *The Rocketeer* were lending their imaginations to the war on terror. They teleconferenced with Army Briga-dier General Kenneth Bergquist, coordinator of special operations units for the military. The meetings were organized by the University of Southern California Institute for Creative Technologies, tasked to create virtual real-ity training for soldiers. Would the competition prompt al Qaeda to consult with Bollywood or studios in Tehran?

Hollywood might help America even more by cleaning up its act. As Michael Medved pointed out in *USA Today*, October 14, 2001, Hollywood's fascination with the dark side of human nature did much to shape Ameri-ca's ugly image in much of the world. Surveys reported in September 2002, showed that 17-year-olds in many countries had extremely negative views of violence and materialism in the U.S. Their main source of information was Hollywood. Those who knew the U.S. mainly through its films would see little of the fundamental decency, generosity and religious feeling that remained part of the American ethos, even though Jimmy Stewart, Katharyn Hepburn and Spencer Tracy no longer graced the silver screen.

"This foreign policy stuff is a little frustrating."

George W. Bush
April 23, 2002

Chapter 10

WASHINGTON'S BIPOLAR DISORDERS: CHINA AND RUSSIA

The Bush team for international security was not manic depressive, but it did suffer from two bipolar disorders. First, some team leaders seemed to need and want a foreign bogy to replace the now deceased USSR. When Dubya brought them back to Washington, Donald Rumsfeld and Dick Cheney looked around for another lodestar to mobilize the nation's energies. China could fill the void. While Clinton had treated China as a potential strategic partner, Dubya's team treated it as a likely peer rival—a surrogate for the old evil empire. The team's arrogant and often aggressive ways served to alarm, antagonize and alienate any Chinese who hoped for some kind of peaceful collaboration with America. As for Russia, Dubya's foreign policy team tended to ignore or insult what was still the world's largest country and potentially one of the richest. Thus, while losing friends in Europe, the Bush administration inspired potential foes across Eurasia.

Second, the team's outlook swung from irrational negativity to irrational exuberance about the prospects of U.S. collaboration with China and/or Russia. Neither country merited America's utter disdain or confidence. Each was a potential powerhouse able to harm the U.S. or work with America to mutual advantage. China had the world's largest population and, in recent years, the world's highest rate of economic growth. Russia still occupied the world's largest territory and retained a vast nuclear arsenal, increasingly vulnerable to misuse or theft.

The events of September 11, 2001, led Washington to shift overnight from very cool to very warm toward Beijing and Moscow. And so Dubya's team, though schooled in Cold War anti-communism, became silent about many Chinese and Russian actions offensive to most Americans—from repression of minorities, religion and the media to destructive environmental policies. Despite Washington's ostensible devotion to democracy, Bushies paid little attention to the reality that China was still unfree in most dimensions; Russia, just partly free. Each country, still ruled by an iron or velvet-over-iron fist, might prove incapable of meeting the complex challenges of the early 21st century. Each could still implode.

TRADE = PEACE?

Americans and Chinese became dependent upon each other—mostly as buyer and seller. The strong flow of consumer goods from China to the U.S. was slightly offset by the sale of Boeing aircraft and other high tech American products to China. Admission to the World Trade Organization in December 2001, committed Beijing to opening its markets to a wide range of foreign products, including agricultural goods, banking and other services. Perhaps China and the United States would grow together to mutual advantage. If both sides were wise and skillful, they could harmonize their complementary needs and assets. But trade could not ensure peace. Germany and Russia had been each other's major trading partners in 1914 and 1940.

CHINA'S BIPOLAR PROBLEM

China, too, suffered bipolar disorders. Should it be open and on-line or closed to the world? What sort of system prevailed in China? Was it communism? Capitalism? A little of each—Leninist capitalism? Communists maintained a one-party dictatorship and state ownership of basic industries. Many branches of the armed forces scored huge profits by wheeling and dealing in high tech ventures. Some Chinese hoped the Internet would help liberalize China. But Chinese authorities sought to maintain mind controls. After a fire killed dozens in an Internet cafe in 2001, police shut off access to the Web for some 6,000 Internet cafes. Later, Beijing authorities allowed

30 cafes to reopen after they pledged to follow fire codes, keep records of computer use for 60 days and install filters to keep out pornography and politically subversive messages. In 2001, eight newspapers were also shut down, including the Nanjing-based *Business Morning Daily*, after it reported President Jiang Zemin had given preferential treatment to Shanghai, where he had strong roots. Some 150 editors were summoned to Beijing and told not to report on major corruption scandals or proposals for political reform.

MORE THAN TÊTE-À-TÊTE

China and the United States in the 21st century might cooperate in many domains. Alternatively, they could compete as bitter rivals. The Bush team seemed to lack any sense that its words could shape which alternative prevailed. Even before he took office, Dubya informed the world that he did not see China as a strategic partner with the United States but as a competitor. After Bush's inauguration, the Pentagon began to shift forces from Europe to Asia. In March 2001, China announced an 18% year-on-year rise in defense spending to $17 billion about one-fifteenth of annual Pentagon outlays prior to 9/11.

On April Fools Day 2001, a Chinese fighter trailing an American EP-3E reconnaissance aircraft collided with it. The Chinese pilot died, becoming a Chinese hero, while the U.S. plane made an emergency landing on China's

Hainan Island. Showing how prophecies can be self-fulfilling, Bush's hostile remarks about China in previous months bolstered the chances that an incident such as this would turn a troubled relationship into a serious confrontation.

NO TAKE-OUTS NEEDED

The American crew was detained on Hainan for questioning and not released until April 12. Beijing claimed that the spy plane had violated Chinese sovereignty. For the Chinese, the event was just another in a chain of Western assaults such as bombing their embassy in Belgrade and other intrusions that went back years, decades and even centuries. The Americans maintained that the incident happened over international waters and that they had a right to fly there, without harassment. Neither side made any effort to refer the dispute to the International Court of Justice for a ruling. Both the Chinese and the Bush team preferred to interpret international law for themselves or ignore it altogether.

Washington demanded the immediate return of the plane, but the Chinese wanted a much closer look. The American crew tried to destroy their communications and spy equipment before landing on Hainan but had little time to complete the job. As the cartoons suggest, Washington initially took the posture of *demandeur*, but shifted toward that of supplicant.

A LOOSE CANNON VS. DIPLOMATIC AMBIGUITY

On April 24, 2001, as the crisis over the spy plane wound down, Washington announced the largest sale of arms to Taiwan in a decade. The package included eight diesel submarines and four frigates. All three capitals—Beijing, Taipei and Washington—had long concurred that there is only "one China." But the potential for an armed confrontation grew in the 1990s as China built up its forces along the Taiwan Strait and threatened war if Taiwan declared its independent statehood. On April 26, 2001, adding fuel to the fires, Mr. Bush told a talk-show host that the U.S. would defend Taiwan with "whatever it takes"—a one-man extension of U.S. alliance policy that could mean war with mainland China. Without consulting Congress or U.S. allies, a loose cannon shattered what had long been a deliberately ambiguous commitment. In May 2001, Dubya set tempers on edge when he received the Dalai Lama at the White House—a man denounced in Beijing for promoting Tibetan separatism, what he termed "autonomy." In 2002-2004, Beijing continued to build up across from Taiwan what it called a capacity for "unlimited war."

WHERE CHINA TAKES FIRST PLACE

China surpassed even Texas in per capita executions each year—probably killing more accused criminals than all other countries combined. Many were condemned for drug dealing, tax evasion, fraud or corrupt practices in banking; some were said to have abused Communist Party privileges. Mass sentencing rallies educated or titillated thousands of spectators before

the condemned were led away. Sometimes relatives had to pay for the bullet—often a shot to the head—so as not to disturb the kidneys and other organs immediately slashed from the victim for use by others. In 2001, a defecting doctor told the U.S. Congress that he had helped remove corneas and harvest skin from more than 100 executed prisoners including one who was still alive. In late 2001, authorities began using lethal injections, said to be much cheaper and less messy than bullets in the head, and probably better for some organ transplants.

A JUDGE OF CHARACTER

For six months after his inauguration, Dubya treated the Russian Federation and Vladimir Putin, the former spy elected RF president in 2000, as nonentities. However, the United States took sufficient interest in its old rival to expel four Russian diplomats for spying in March 2001, and demanded that

Moscow withdraw another 46 by July 1—the largest such action since 1986, when President Reagan ordered 80 Soviet diplomats to leave. Washington was miffed to find that former FBI agent Robert Hanssen had delivered highly sensitive information to his Kremlin handlers for more than 15 years. Russian officials complained that Bush was returning to Cold War thinking and retaliated by expelling 50 Americans.

Having met Putin face-to-face in Slovenia in June 2001, however, Dubya claimed to have discovered in the ex-KGB agent's eyes a leader with whom the United States could partner. Skeptics remembered the song *Ochi chornye* ["Dark eyes"] and wondered if Americans could or should cooperate with a man whose popularity in Russia seemed to rest on his pursuing another of Russia's genocidal wars in Chechnya.

COLD WAR IS PASSÉ

After meeting Putin, Dubya declared: "Russia is no longer our enemy, and therefore we shouldn't be locked into a Cold War mentality that says we keep the peace by blowing each other up. In my attitude, that's old, that's tired, that's stale." When Russian officials complained that Washington planned to scuttle the 1972 ABM treaty, however, the Bush team gave them a "like it or lump it" response. The ABM treaty, Bushies said, was a Cold War relic. America and world security needed an anti-missile defense to fend off attacks by rogue nations and terrorists.

GLASNOST CLOSING

Russia and China developed mind-control long before Texas test-book screeners. Putin built on a long tradition. Russian leaders, like Chinese leaders, claimed their most urgent job was to maintain order. Without stability, they argued, economic progress would be impossible. Putin wanted to modernize Russia economically but tighten controls over the media. He cowed much of the provincial press by wielding the government's control over office rents, paper supplies and postage rates.

In Soviet times many Russians were avid newspaper readers, seeking enlightenment by reading between the lines. Too poor to buy newspapers in the 1990s, most Russians got their news from TV. President Putin, however, put the main TV channels under government control. In October 2002, he annulled a decree issued by Boris Yeltsin in 1991 allowing Radio Free Europe/Radio Liberty to operate permanent offices in Moscow and elsewhere in Russia. "We are becoming a closed society," said the chairman of the Glasnost Defense Foundation. Without even one TV channel that offered an alternative to Putin's world view, democracy did not exist. Election outcomes were manipulated from on-high. Bush's dear friend in the Kremlin assigned former KGB officers to occupy half of the top jobs in the Russian power structure.

CAN A LUBE JOB SMOOTH OVER GENOCIDE?

Could oil smooth away all the rough spots—even Putin's genocidal campaign in Chechnya? Bush's desire to reduce U.S. dependency on Middle Eastern oil added to Russia's luster. But the most immediate reason for closer U.S. relations with Russia was a shared interest in containing Islamic militants. The events of 9/11 pushed the Bush administration to do an about-face. Washington no longer kept its distance from Beijing and Moscow. Instead, the United States embraced China and Russia as partners against a shared adversary.[1]

Yes, the United States continued a military buildup worrisome to Chinese and Russian planners. And it now wanted bases in Central Asia close to Chinese as well as Russian borders. But nearly everything that Beijing and Moscow did that offended American ideals or threatened U.S. interests was forgiven, forgotten or ignored.

Beijing, too, disliked the Taliban and wanted Washington to keep quiet about Chinese treatment of Uighurs and Kazaks in Xinjiang where China's greatest oil deposits resided. Far from condemning China's treatment of its minorities or Russia's war against Chechens, the White House discovered that Muslim separatists resisting Chinese and Russian rule had some ties with al Qaeda—the perfect pretext for repressive measures by Beijing and Moscow.

Washington alternated frosty and warm toward Beijing and Moscow. In October 2001, meeting for the first time, Presidents Jiang Zemin and Bush agreed to work toward a "constructive relationship of cooperation"—less than a "strategic partnership" but more cordial than "strategic competition." But in January 2002, the United States imposed sanctions on three Chinese firms it accused of supplying Iran with materials that could be used in making chemical and biological weapons.

President Dubya had declared that Russia was no longer an enemy of the United States. But the administration's January 2002, *Nuclear Posture Review* stated that a nuclear contingency with Russia was still "plausible" though "not expected." It warned that if America's "relations with Russia significantly worsen in the future, the U.S. may need to revise its nuclear force levels and posture."

Russia's major ethnic challenge—Chechnya—helped bring Presidents Putin and Bush together after 9/11. Putin characterized the Chechens as bandits paid for by al Qaeda. So he and the U.S. had a common enemy, he claimed. Following the Moscow hostage crisis in late 2002, Putin loosened the reins on Russian troops in Chechnya. Result: More young Chechen men were rounded up in their villages at night, tortured, butchered and thrown in garbage dumps.[2] In February 2004, Putin's government took offense when Qatar arrested two Russian secret service agents for assassinating a Chechen exile who had once been president of the break-away republic. Qatar released a third assassin because he carried a diplomatic passport.

NEWFOUND INTIMACIES
(MACHIAVELLI WOULD SMILE)

Old habits die hard. Bureaucracies do their thing. Chinese as well as Russian spies had long been active in the United States. Americans had a more difficult time penetrating Chinese and Russian secrecy and so relied heavily on technology. Thus, in January 2002, China's president found that a plane custom-made for him in the United States was full of bugging devices. No official apologies or accusations were exchanged. Realpolitik triumphed over righteous indignation. A big Chinese protest would expose Jiang to charges he had been suckered.

A MEETING OF BODIES
BUT NOT OF MINDS

Visiting China in February 2002—thirty years after President Nixon toasted Mao Zedong in Beijing—Bush pressed China to halt arms shipments to Iraq, Iran, North Korea, Syria and Pakistan. When the U.S. established bases in Kyrgyzstan and Uzbekistan to deal with Afghanistan, the Chinese nervously acquiesced. But Beijing warned Dubya not to attack Iraq. The Chinese president sang "*O Sole Mio*" for Bush and danced with "Condi" at a banquet, but the two sides reached no new agreements. Bush refused to reaffirm his commitment to the three U.S.-Chinese accords of the 1970s and 1980s that Beijing regarded as laying down the basis for relations between the two states. Instead, Bush pledged his support for the 1979 Taiwan Relations Act committing the United States to help Taiwan maintain its ability to defend itself against any attack by the mainland. Meanwhile, the U.S. was arming Taiwan against China and again courting Pakistan, a major partner of China.

BUSH'S REWARD FOR APPEASING
BEIJING ON XINJIANG AND TAIWAN

Point and counterpoint: In March 2002, U.S. Deputy Secretary of Defense Paul Wolfowitz met Taiwan's Minister of Defense for two days of talks in Florida (not so "official" as Washington, D.C.). Despite this offense to Beijing's sensibilities, the man destined soon to become China's president, Ho Jintao, visited President Bush in Washington in April 2002. And June

2002, saw a U.S. delegation visit Beijing to explore a possible resumption of military-to-military contacts. In August 2002, however, after Deputy Secretary of State Richard Armitage went to China and agreed to recognize a separatist group in Xinjiang as a terrorist entity, Beijing promptly expressed its gratitude by test firing a DF-4 missile which, with its 4,000 plus mile range, could wipe Guam off the map.

In late 2003, the president veered again. He made a low kow-tow to Beijing and urged Taiwan not to hold a referendum on whether China should pull back the missiles it had targeted on the island. So much for principles such as self-defense and self-rule!

A HOLEY ALLIANCE

May 2002: Having signed a treaty pledging to reduce their nuclear arsenals by two-thirds by 2012, Presidents Bush and Putin traveled from Russia to Italy. There, at a heavily guarded air base near Rome, the leaders of NATO's nineteen member countries and President Putin signed an accord creating a NATO-Russia Council supposed to give Moscow an equal voice on a wide range of issues such as counter-terrorism, peacekeeping and arms control. President Bush said this was an historic achievement that would establish peace and freedom across Europe. In some ways the accord resembled the Holy Alliance proposed by Tsar Alexander I in 1815 to maintain peace and order in Europe. Such pledges are sometimes difficult to implement. Thus, Dubya's team complained in Summer 2002, that Russia was continuing to build up Iran's nuclear capacity and that Moscow tilted toward Baghdad.

Having sneered at Bill Clinton's personal diplomacy with Putin's predecessor, Boris Yeltsin, Bush met often with Putin. In 2002, the two leaders signed a strategic arms reduction treaty. At U.S. insistence, however, the treaty permitted each side to keep—not destroy—the warheads withdrawn from their arsenal for future contingencies. The U.S. agreed with Russia to reduce its arsenal of long-range nuclear weapons from 6000 to about 2000, but it would store—not destroy—dismantled warheads. The *Nuclear Posture Review* also allowed that, in certain circumstances, the United States might fight China with nuclear weapons.

XENOPHOBIA + FASCISM = ?

Facing strong opposition in the UN to its Iraq war, Washington developed a policy: "Punish France, Ignore Germany and Forgive Russia." This orientation, according to Soviet-born world chess champion Garry Kaspirov was one of the worst blunders made by the U.S. in recent years—one that he attributed to Dr. Rice. The policy gave Putin a green light to escalate the war in Chechnya and to stage a Soviet-style referendum there—all dissenting voices excluded. Kaspirov continued: "The collapse of infant democracy in Russia is contrary to vital U.S. interests. With *de facto* liquidation of the institution of a free press (hardly noticed by the U.S. State Department) and increasing power of the former KGB, now called the FSB, Russia is increasingly overloaded with anti-U.S. hysteria. State-controlled media have been competing with the ultra-nationalistic press in slamming American policies right, left and center. All this is breeding xenophobia and fascism."[3]

XENOPHOBIA + FASCISM + ANTISEMITISM = THE PRESIDENCY

In October 2003, the Putin regime whisked the head of Russia's largest privately owned oil company, Yukos, from his private plane to a jail cell, accusing him of financial irregularities. Mikhail Khodorkovsky had dared to finance voices of opposition to Putin. One of the firm's major shareholders,

Platon Lebedev, was also jailed. The Kremlin signaled to Russia's oligarchs (most of them of Jewish descent) that they could get rich but should stay out of politics. All around the country, businesses were harassed on orders of local authorities. Independent journalists were sued and even imprisoned for criticizing members of local administrations.

Dubya's good friend Vladimir was consolidating his dictatorship. Putin's favorite party, United Russia, took over Russia's lower house in December 2003, in an election that international observers called distorted. As neither liberal party won even 5% of the vote, they lost all representation in the Duma. Putin discharged his PM and the entire cabinet a month before the March 2004, presidential elections with barely a cavil or complaint from his groveling or indifferent subjects. The new PM had worked in foreign trade but he was also a security specialist who had headed the tax police. By America's November-December 2000, standard, however, who could cast the first stone? [4]

V. Putin, Mr. Bush's friend in Moscow

"I understand that the unrest in the Middle East creates unrest throughout the region."

George W. Bush
March 13, 2002

Chapter 11

"HONEST BROKERING" IN THE "HOLY LAND"

Nowhere was official Washington's split personality more evident than in its approach to the Middle East. American policy suffered from two internal contradictions. First, Dubya's team curried the favor of two very different audiences. It lusted for the votes and money of those Christians and Jews who believed Israel could do no wrong. But it also wooed and protected the sheikdoms whose oil wells fed the gasoline pumps of Europe, Japan and the United States. Besides, the fortunes of the Bush dynasty and many of their associates depended on oil or gas. Since the Palestinians had neither, their interests suffered.

The second contradiction divided diplomats led by Colin Powell willing to give dialogue a chance—even with Yasser Arafat—from unilateralists like Donald Rumsfeld who advised Israel and the United States to depend on brute force. Powell sought coalitions of willing partners; Rumsfeld *et al.* were far more inclined to go it alone. Rumsfeld was a pragmatist but his deputy Paul Wolfowitz and adviser Richard Perle seemed also to have an ideological agenda.[1] Perle also had a profit agenda: He advised the Israeli government as well as the U.S. even as he headed businesses that fed at the Pentagon trough.

Besides these elements, as we shall see, there were also American Zionists—both Christian and Jewish. Orchestrating the concert was Karl Rove—ever searching for votes and money to keep Dubya in power. All this made for a weird and frothy brew.

As long as these contradictions persisted, U.S. policy toward the Middle East could never be coherent or effective. Americans were torn between sentiment and power. Most Americans felt that Jews, survivors of pogroms and the Holocaust, should again have their own homeland. On the other hand, geopolitics pushed Washington to court the oil sheiks. Washington claimed to be "even handed," but seemed to favor Israel, though collaborating behind the scenes with Kuwait and Saudi Arabia. The pro-Israeli tilt was expensive. Ever since 1979, Israel got the lion's share of U.S. foreign aid, leaving little for others' pressing needs. Even more damaging, America's pro-Israeli bias antagonized Muslims across the world and inspired jihadists determined to harm the United States.

"PERFIDIOUS ALBION" PLANTS SEEDS OF CONFLICT

The religious faiths born in the Middle East inspire much of the best and the worst that people do with and to each other. Conflicts among Jews, Christians and Muslims have been less about theology and more about land—sacred places as well as fields and fountains. European Christians crusaded to recover the Holy Land but, after many battles, they retreated. When Christians forced Jews out of Spain and other parts of Europe, however, many found refuge in Muslim lands. Jews and Muslims achieved a *modus vivendi* until the British placed spiders among tarantulas. By 1914, London wielded great influence from Persia to Egypt. Seeking support in World War I, the British promised Jews land they had already pledged to Arabs, only to take it later for themselves. In 1916, London promised Hussein, Sharif of Mecca, an independent state in the Arab provinces of the Ottoman Empire. In 1917, Britain assured Zionists a "national home for the Jewish people" in Palestine. Meanwhile, London schemed with Paris to partition the Ottoman realm. In 1920, the British placed sons of Hussein on the thrones of Iraq and Trans-Jordan, each a British client-state, but took Palestine as a British protectorate, while France got Syria and Lebanon. Such double, triple, or quintuple dealing won London the nickname "Perifidious Albion."

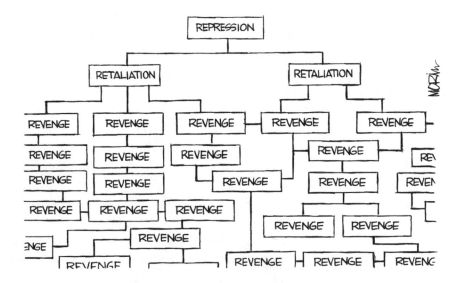

The Middle East Family Tree...

WHOSE ORANGE GROVES? WHOSE STATE?

Britain's perfidy continued. In 1939, London announced it had fulfilled its commitment to Jews and tried to restrict Jewish immigration and land purchases in Palestine. After World War II, Britain tried in vain to prevent an exodus of Jews to Palestine. Exhausted, Britain withdrew from Palestine in 1947, leaving a land in turmoil. Arabs wanted one Palestinian state, but a UN majority voted to create a Jewish *and* an Arab state in Palestine, with Jerusalem internationalized. In 1948, communal violence flared. Israel declared its independence and repulsed invading Arab armies. Many Palestinians sought refuge in neighboring lands. After the 1967 war, Israel controlled not just the Sinai and Golan Heights, but also all of Jerusalem, the Jordan River's West Bank and the Gaza Strip—what Palestinians then called the Occupied Territories. The Palestinian diaspora multiplied but most Palestinians remained stateless, living in nearby countries. How could they return to their families' orange groves without obliterating the Jewishness of Israel?

Many Arabs and Jews wanted to coexist in peace, but extremists on both sides stood ready—with stones, bombs and bullets—to attack peacemakers ready to compromise. Rights and wrongs abounded. Each side found justification for its suspicions and tough actions toward the other.

THE BUSH AND SAUDI
DYNASTIES ENRICH EACH OTHER

Oil smudged the vision and judgment of George I and II and their entourage. Dick Cheney amassed some $60 million as CEO of Halliburton before he resigned to run for VP. In July 2000, candidate Cheney claimed that his policy had been to keep Halliburton from doing "anything in Iraq, even—even arrangements that were supposedly legal." But the *Washington Post* discovered that, on Cheney's watch, Halliburton subsidiaries had signed contracts to deliver $73 million in oil equipment to Iraq—legal under the UN oil-for-food program.

Dubya's Secretary of Commerce Donald Evans had accumulated $24 million as CEO of Tom Brown, Inc., a small but profitable oil and gas firm. Bush's chief of staff Andrew H. Card, Jr., had led a $25 million lobbying campaign by Detroit's Big Three against higher mileage requirements. The Secretary of the Army and other high officials had their Enron connections. Only one current Bush aid had an oil tanker named for her—Condoleezza Rice, a board member of the Chevron Corporation since 1991, though former Washington officials George Shultz and David Packard also had Chevron tankers named for them.

AMERICA'S CHRISTIAN ZIONISTS

The Middle East has no monopoly on zealotry. The National Unity Coalition for Israel, claiming to represent 40 million Evangelical Christians, Catholics and Jews, attacked Bill Clinton for allegedly siding with Palestinians against Israel. After 9/11, the Capital Hill Prayer Alert (CHPA) issued an alert slogan: "It's a Holy War! How to Pray for George W. Bush." On August 7, 2002, Roberta Combs, President of the Christian Coalition of America, praised Secretary of Defense Rumsfeld for protecting America's only ally in the Middle East, Israel. "There has been too much talk of a Palestinian state," said Combs. She praised Rumsfeld for declining to characterize the West Bank as occupied territory. According to Combs, Rumsfeld in a Pentagon briefing opined "it's hard to know" whether Jewish communities there should be dismantled as part of a so-called peace process. The coalition held a Christian Solidarity with Israel Rally on October 11, 2002, at Washington's Ellipse. Invited speakers included Benjamin Netanyahu, Pat Robertson, Oliver North, Allan Keyes and Ms. Combs. The coalition web page announcing this event showed a red-white-and-blue five pointed star fused with a blue-and-white star of David.

IMBALANCES OF TERROR

Looking at these cartoons, a 23-year old Palestinian poet said: "I can see that you try to be objective—to show that each side bears responsibility. But we cannot be objective. They took our lands and still hold them. What if the Soviet Union had seized your land instead of just challenging your ideology? Could you be objective about who started the Cold War?"

Indeed, Americans found it hard to empathize. Why could not Israelis and Palestinians come to terms like Ronald Reagan and Mikhail Gorbachev? But very few Americans and Soviets had died fighting each other. No Americans dreamed of recovering an orange grove taken by Soviet interlopers.

Reagan and Gorbachev negotiated about a balance of terror. But the face-off between Israel and its neighbors was unsteady, fluid, uneven. Arab states had many more soldiers, but Israeli military training and equipment were superior. Israel's ace was its "Samson option"—nuclear weapons that could pull down the roof. Many Palestinians were well educated, but Israel had shredded their economic life. More than half lived as exiles—often stateless. Some Palestinian Arabs were Israeli citizens; others lived under Israeli occupation. Their ace was suicide bombers. It is not clear that Chairman Arafat ordered suicide bombings in the early 21st century, but he probably welcomed some and lamented others, depending on what he deemed expedient at the time.

BETTER LATE THAN NEVER?

The Bush team shunned the "honest broker" role played by many U.S. leaders throughout the 20th century. In 1905 and 1906, President Theodore Roosevelt used his good offices to end the Russo-Japanese War and to defuse a German-French confrontation over Morocco. Former State Department official Ralph Bunche, having joined the UN Secretariat, mediated

a ceasefire between Israel and Egypt in 1949. Henry Kissinger practiced "shuttle diplomacy" after the 1973 Arab-Israeli wars. Jimmy Carter mediated Egyptian-Israeli peace in 1978-1979. In 2000, Bill Clinton brokered the best terms Israel ever offered the Palestinians. For most of 2001, however, Dubya refused to offer the good offices of the U.S. to others to resolve their disputes except in the Caucasus, where Armenia's conflict with Azerbaijan threatened Chevron's efforts to pump and pipe Azeri and Kazak oil.

After 9/11 and the U.S. counterattack on terrorism, Washington sought a more constructive role in resolving Israeli-Palestinian differences. By the time Mr. Powell got to the West Bank in 2002, however, Israeli forces had leveled the homes of many Palestinians and smashed much of the local infrastructure.

DIALOGUE

Responding to an upsurge in Palestinian bombings, the Israeli Defense Force (IDF) reoccupied much of the West Bank and Gaza starting on March 1, 2002. After Israelis killed more than a dozen civilians in Gaza while assassinating a leader of Hamas, some Israeli parliamentarians condemned their government for using weapons that were bound to do enormous collateral damage. In June 2002, IDF blew up part of a large PLO building in Hebron. Still, there had been no massacres—and certainly no genocide. A UN study found that the number of Palestinians killed when Israel reoccupied Hebron

was closer to 50 than to 500. The IDF demolished 878 civilian homes as well as buildings belonging to the Palestinian Authority. Meanwhile, 16 more terrorist attacks killed more than 100 Israelis.

DICTATED DEMOCRACY

Many Americans believed that the U.S. had done its best to protect Chairman Arafat over the years. In 1982, the U.S. had helped him escape from Lebanon, besieged by Israelis, to Tunisia. In 1993, President Clinton encouraged a handshake between Arafat and Israeli Prime Minster Yitzhak Rabin in the White House Rose Garden. President George W. urged Israel not to kill Arafat when Israeli troops surrounded his compound in 2002. From the Palestinian standpoint, however, the United States was far from even-handed. Official and unofficial aid from the U.S. to Israel ran to billions each year. Israeli forces repeatedly struck Palestinian targets with U.S. planes and tanks.

In 2002, Prime Minister Sharon and President Bush demanded that Palestinians find a new leader to replace Yasser Arafat. Though Dubya said he wanted democracy for Palestinians, he told them their most popular leader was not acceptable. Israel destroyed some Palestinian Authority buildings and limited Arafat's movements. Sharon talked of exiling him. Chairman Arafat responded by allowing other Palestinians to serve as "prime minister," but then undermined them by retaining control of the security forces.

DO WALLS WORK?

Both Bush and Sharon ignored the history of failed defenses: Joshua overcame the walls of Jericho. Mongols penetrated the Great Wall and ruled China for centuries. Germans skirted the Maginot Line in 1940. The allies broke through Hitler's Siegfried Line in 1945. Flying through Soviet air defenses on the "Day of the Border Guards" in 1987, a single-engine German civilian plane landed in Red Square. Berliners tore down the Communist Wall with bare hands in 1989. Terrorists steered U.S. airliners into the Pentagon and World Trade Center on 9/11. Despite it all, Dubya demanded an antimissile defense even though America's foes could deliver mass destruction weapons by suitcase, ship or truck. For his part, Sharon ordered a long wall to keep Palestinians out of Israel proper. The barricade separated Palestinian families and prevented some farmers from reaching their fields. It was also a land-grab—shrinking Palestinian territory. By Christmas 2003, even Bethlehem

was being sealed off. President Bush said "tut-tut" and cut off a few million from billions of U.S. aid to Israel. Would the wall prevent militant Palestinians from harming Israelis or energize their drive to do so?

Starting in March 2003, the President backed a "road map" for peace in the Middle East, a plan co-sponsored by the EU, Russia and the UN. According to the plan's timetable, a Palestinian state with provisional borders would be established by the end of the year, with full statehood coming within three years. When the road hit the usual bumps and the 2004 elections loomed, Dubya's firm commitment disappeared.

Chapter 12

JIHADS→CRUSADES→JIHADS→?

Could 9/11 have been prevented? The Bush team ignored myriad warnings that terrorists might attack the U.S. with civilian airliners or other weapons.[1] Once the attack took place, Dubya responded by mobilizing what he called a "crusade"—later changed to "war"—against "evil." He did almost nothing to analyze or remove the sources of anti-American sentiment. Indeed, most of his actions fanned this hatred. He claimed that the terrorists were against "freedom," but Osama bin Laden talked only about the U.S. presence in Saudi Arabia and U.S. support for Israel. Making a bad situation worse, Dubya's response to 9/11 bulldozed many constitutional protections of civil and political liberty, as we see in the next chapter.

Did the Bush team invade Afghanistan to destroy bin Laden or to win the next elections? Was Osama, his kidneys dependent on dialysis, really in Afghanistan?[2] Or did he send his cave-scene videos from an air-conditioned suite in some Arab capital?

The Bush team seemed more solicitous of the feelings of Saudi elites than of the rights and security of Americans. In the days after the 9/11 attacks, and while U.S. skies were still closed to civilian traffic, the White House permitted private planes to collect two dozen bin Ladens from around the U.S. and then fly them away from U.S. interrogators, despite evidence of high-level Saudi support for anti-American activity.[3]

Skeptics wondered: Who really did this and why? Could it just happen that the personal documents of reputed 9/11 leader Mohammed Atta would surface in the debris of the World Trade Center? Why did Atta leave his will in an auto at the Boston airport? Could amateur pilots with minimal training steer three huge Boeing aircraft into the five-story Pentagon and the not-so-wide N.Y. towers?[4] Or was this the work of professional pilots—like the Egyptian who nose-dived his airliner into the ocean off Nantucket in 1999?[5]

To ask such questions is to think the nearly unthinkable, except that the Bush team had shown itself to have no scruples in the pursuit of wealth and power. Consider, for example, how it savaged John McCain—arguably America's greatest war hero—in the 2000 South Carolina primaries[6], or its subsequent revelation that the wife of whistle-blower Joseph Wilson was a high level CIA agent.[7] Suspicions arose in part because the White House stonewalled Congressional investigators asking what the administration knew before 9/11 and when it knew it—a stonewall even more serious than the refusal to admit the makeup of Cheney's energy task force.

OTHER PRIORITIES DELAYED
ACTION AGAINST AL QAEDA

Alibis proliferated faster than weapons. Dr. Rice avowed: "Had this president known of something more specific or known that a plane was going to be used as a missile, he would have acted on it." Bush allowed that "second guessing has become second nature."

Time reported in August 2002, that the Bush administration had spurned an action plan suggested by the interagency Counter-Terrorism Security Group (CSG) in January 2001. The CSG proposed a plan to "roll back" al Qaeda instead of waiting for its next strike. The CSG wanted to break up al Qaeda cells, arrest personnel, undermine or freeze its finances, assist countries like the Philippines to fight terrorists, destroy al Qaeda training camps in Afghanistan and back anti-Taliban forces in Afghanistan. But the

CSG plan had evolved in the 1990s and the Bush team wanted "anything but Clinton." Dubya's first priority was tax relief, but in security affairs his team wanted modernization of the armed forces, a national missile defense, and preparations to deal with China. The Bush team carried out its own study of terrorism and adopted a strategy to eliminate al Qaeda, but the plan was not approved until September 4—one week before the 9/11 disasters.

WHY HATE INFIDELS?

You have to be taught
To hate and fear
You have to be taught
From year to year,
It's got to be drummed
In your dear little ear
You have to be carefully taught.

You've got to be taught to be afraid
Of people whose eyes are oddly made,
And people whose skin is a different shade,
You've got to be carefully taught.

You've got to be taught before it's too late,
Before you are six or seven or eight,
To hate all the people your relatives hate,
You've got to be carefully taught!

—Rogers and Hammerstein, *South Pacific*

For centuries, Islamic culture had failed to meet the challenges of a changing world. In the late 20th century, Islamic societies produced little except oil and hate. From Saudi Arabia and Yemen to Pakistan and Indonesia, "madrassa" schools trained young people, mostly boys, to memorize the *Koran* in classical Arabic. With rote religion usually came political indoctrination—sometimes quite militant and self-righteous. Madrassa training aimed at the spirit, but was often grounded in economics. Poor families in Pakistan and other countries sent their sons to madrassas to be fed as well as to receive some kind of education. Many of them became the foot soldiers of jihad.[8]

DYNASTIC MARRIAGES

In 1990-1991, George the Elder led a broad UN coalition that saved Kuwait from Iraq and gave the country an opportunity to liberalize. Ten years later, however, civil liberties and women's rights in Kuwait were still very constrained. A 1999 royal decree granting women the right to vote was defeated in parliament, where Islamicists and other traditionals outvoted modernizers. In the early 21st century more Kuwait women were veiling their faces.

After 9/11, many Kuwaitis condemned U.S. attacks on the Taliban, but Kuwait's government endorsed the Afghan war. It stripped a spokesman for al Qaeda of his Kuwaiti citizenship and curtailed private Kuwaiti donations to al Qaeda "charities."

Assisting Kuwait against Saddam's aggression seemed noble. But how much of this solidarity was "fueled" by the Bush dynasty's business ties with Arab sheiks? Even Dubya's first oil venture, "Arbusto," as well as the follow-on Harken, had Middle East financing. Former Secretary of State James Baker represented Saudi royals (including their defense against 9/11 claimants) as well as the Bushes (as in the 2000 Florida fiasco). Baker was also a principal in the Carlyle Group—a leading element in the U.S. military-industrial complex, in which Saudis had invested and where George the Elder "consulted."

CULTURAL RELATIVISM: T-SHIRTS
AS JUSTIFICATION FOR RAPE

Village culture in most of Afghanistan, Pakistan and Iran accepted that a woman's place is in the home. The Taliban's Department for the Propagation of Virtue banned women from walking in the street unless accompanied by a male relative. Its agents beat women who displayed a wisp of hair or an inch of ankle. Nor did the Taliban's major foe, the Northern Alliance, champion women's-lib. Its troops practiced orgies of rape, mass murder and pillage in the 1990s.

After the Taliban left, many Afghan women still feared to remove the burka. An instructor in female rights explained: "A rapist cannot attack an Afghan woman if she doesn't provide the opportunity. If she goes out in a T-shirt or skimpy clothes among men who are used to seeing women covered, they will think she's immoral. If something were to happen to her, it would be seen as her own fault."

CULTURAL ABSOLUTISM
(USEFUL HINTS FOR TEXANS?)

A month or so before 9/11, the Taliban's religious police arrested eight for-eign relief workers—Germans, Americans and Australians—and sixteen of their Afghan associates on suspicion of trying to spread Christianity, a crime punishable by death under the Taliban's version of Islamic law. The evidence included Christian literature in Dari. All the detainees were employed by Shelter Now International, based in Wisconsin. At first the Taliban refused requests by foreign diplomats to visit the detainees, but then magnanimously offered visas to the International Red Cross and to diplomats based in Islam-abad. A Taliban representative in Pakistan explained that Mohammed was the last prophet "so automatically any other religion does not exist," and any Muslim who converts to another religion must be punished by death. The Taliban's Deputy Minister for the Promotion of Virtue and Prevention of Vice said that 59 children taught by the outsiders had been sent to "a correc-tion house to remove from their hearts and minds the Christian teachings." The vice minister's ideology differed but he might qualify as a mind control consultant to the Texas Foundation for Public Policy or even to Attorney General John Ashcroft.

AFGHAN WARLORDS BETTER
PARTNERS THAN NATO ALLIES?

Though some Palestinians danced in the streets after 9/11, much of human-ity commiserated. "We are all Americans," declared *Le Monde*. The UN Security Council expressed the UN's "readiness to take all necessary steps to respond to the terrorist attacks of 11th September 2001 and to combat all forms of terrorism." NATO issued an unprecedented declaration that

America's war was NATO's. But moral support did not mean military support. Only the UK sent troops. Pakistan permitted use of its air space. Russia acquiesced in the building of U.S. bases in Central Asia. Uzbek President Islam Karimov agreed to let Uzbek territory serve as a launch pad for U.S. operations against the Taliban. The French foreign minister noted that Article 5 of the NATO Charter "does not abolish the freedom of action of each ally." Germany's foreign minister said "hasty action" should be avoided.

The Pentagon, however, liked it this way. Rumsfeld did not want another Kosovo, where every bombing raid had to be cleared with all of NATO. Even after the Taliban was routed, the U.S. did not seek a large international force to establish order.

THE PENTAGON'S REVOLUTION
IN MILITARY TECHNOLOGY

In late October 2001, the Pentagon revealed that a small number of U.S. special operations forces were working closely with members of the Northern Alliance. Some entered Afghanistan at night in low-flying helicopters. Once on the ground, they moved about by foot, in trucks and on horseback. They included air controllers who guided U.S. warplanes to their targets using hand-held lasers and satellite locators. Others helped resistance forces with food, ammunition and communications. Before the uniformed U.S. personnel arrived, CIA agents were conducting liaison work with northern insurgents. The first American to die in the fighting was a CIA agent helping to interrogate Taliban prisoners when they staged an uprising.

The Pentagon saw "smart bombs" as its ace—a way to destroy enemy targets with little "collateral damage" or risk to U.S. lives. In Afghanistan such weapons did not hit any Chinese government offices, as they did in Belgrade during NATO's Kosovo campaign. But U.S. bombs almost killed Washington's chosen leader for Afghanistan, Hamid Karzai, and did destroy an Afghan wedding party along with other non-military targets. Some faulty "guidance" came from ostensibly friendly Afghans who wanted American bombs to wipe out a rival faction.

CULTURAL RELATIVISM ON THE PLAYING FIELD

Afghans, like Americans, claim to prize "freedom," but they may have different views of freedom and order. In American baseball a runner may advance by "stealing" a base, but only under specific rules. In October 2001, several teams from the Northern Alliance played buzkashi, a chaotic version of polo, as they waited to advance on Kabul. Players on horseback fight to possess a dead goat or, in this case, half of a calf. If a warrior can grab the animal's legs, he tries to gallop across the field to a green-and-white flag and then sprint to the other end of the field to deposit the carcass in a hole. His teammates block the other side as huge clouds of dust envelop the riders. Women may not watch. If horses stampede, the crowd scatters. Buzkashi is a favorite sport among the horse cultures of Central Asia. Legend says it is a gift from the time of Genghis Khan when, on occasion, the game was played with a human corpse.

WHAT WILL FOLLOW PSYCH-OPS?

In October 2001, Defense Secretary Rumsfeld confirmed that U.S. planes were dropping propaganda leaflets on Afghanistan. They exhorted Afghans to reject the Taliban and Osama bin Laden. The leaflets were a bit larger than dollar bills so as to encourage a close look. The Voice of America and the BBC added to the chorus of exhortations. Along with bombs, U.S. planes also dropped food packets—37,500 by mid-October. Each packet displayed the stars-and-stripes and announced it was a gift from the U.S.A. President Bush averred that "the oppressed people of Afghanistan will know the generosity of America and our allies. As we strike, we will also drop food, medicine and supplies to the starving and the suffering." Unfortunately, some packets landed in mine fields. Afghanistan's poverty could be summed up in a single statistic: Before the Soviet invasion in December 1979, one in four babies died at birth his or her first year. After that, things got worse.

AFGHANISTAN UNDER U.S. TUTELAGE: #1 IN OPIUM

Great Britain forced China to permit British merchants to sell opium in the 1840s, but London denounced the Taliban in 2001 for ruining the health of young Brits. Tony Blair declared: "The arms the Taliban are buying today are paid for with the lives of young British people buying their drugs on the British streets. That is another part of their regime we should seek to destroy." Yes, opium had long been a part of Afghan life, but the poppy business took off when U.S. and French agents decided to use drugs to weaken Soviet forces in Afghanistan.

When the Taliban won most of Afghanistan in 1996, they taxed the flour-

ishing narco-traffic. Raw material from Afghanistan was converted into mor-
phine and heroin in Turkey. Afghan production doubled from 1996 to 2000,
when Taliban leader Mullah Omar banned all planting for the next season.

In the two years following the collapse of the Taliban 2002-2003, poppy
cultivation soared nearly 20-fold. Eradication and subsidies for alternative
crops failed. Afghanistan under U.S. control regained its title as the world's
leading producer of opium. UN officials worried that Afghanistan could become a failed state controlled by drug lords and narcotraffickers.

THE U.S. ALIGNS WITH ISLAMIC
STATES AGAINST WOMEN'S RIGHTS

There was good news, terrible news and merely bad news about women in
Afghanistan. After 9/11, official Washington took note. In November 2001,
First Lady Laura Bush reported some good news in a radio address from the
White House: "Because of our recent military gains in much of Afghanistan,
women are no longer imprisoned in their homes. They can listen to music
and teach their daughters without fear of punishment." Part of the terrible
news was that some of the 3,000 Afghan women imprisoned for non-Mus-
lim behavior had disappeared from Kabul's Pol-i-Charki prison—perhaps
abducted as sex slaves. The merely bad news was that the U.S. Senate continued its refusal (since 1980!) to approve the Convention on the Elimination
of All Forms of Discrimination Against Women. Would the Bush team push
for its ratification? In Summer 2002, the White House said it needed more
time to study the treaty. The U.S., said Senator Joseph Biden, "has joined
an Axis of Shortsightedness—in the company of Syria, Sudan, Afghanistan
and Iran."

QATAR'S ANSWER TO FOX NEWS

Americans had long complained that in most Islamic societies the government controlled the news media. In 1996 Qatar imported Arabic broad-
casters from the BBC and established al Jazeera TV news, one of the most
free news outlets in the Islamic world. The station pulled its punches about
Qatar, but its reports on other Arab governments were so critical that Qatar's
Foreign Ministry regularly received complaints from its neighbors. But if
Fox and NBC tilted toward Israel and depicted the kinder and gentler aspects
of U.S. operations in Afghanistan, al Jazeera did the opposite. It featured
the blood and tears caused by Israeli and U.S. armed forces. It became the

main outlet by which Osama bin Laden's words and images reached the world. Al Jazeera interviewed Condi Rice but edited the product to undercut her message. The White House urged the U.S. media to be cautious about purchasing al Qaeda propaganda from al Jazeera. Meanwhile, Qatar also headquartered major banks and law firms. It also provided a base for U.S. planes that could attack Iraq.

DUBYA NOT WILD ABOUT HARMONY
WHILE RUMSFELD DEMANDS SOLO

Referring to Clinton's interventions in Somalia and in the Balkans, candidate Bush warned in 2000: "If we don't stop extending our troops all around the world in nation-building missions, then we are going to have a serious problem coming down the road." After driving the Taliban from Kabul and Kandahar, however, the Americans discovered that they had little choice but to engage in nation-building, for there was no indivisible "Afghan" nation, with liberty and justice for all. Instead, there was a land of Pashtuns, Uzbeks and other distinct ethnic groups, each with its own culture and language. The country was more complex than a Persian rug—a tangled weave of regional fiefdoms, tribal and religious rivalries and enemy-of-my-enemy

alliances. Reversing field, President Bush conceded in October 2001, that "we...should learn a lesson from the previous engagement in the Afghan area, that we should not leave after a military objective has been achieved." Condi had to move closer to Colin if they were to play this tune in harmony. But Rumsfeld controlled most of the relevant resources and he preferred to play solo.

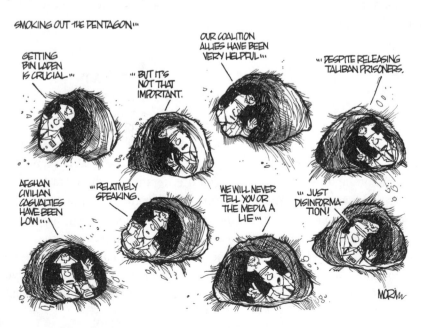

KARZAI COLLECTS MILLIONS
BUT NEEDS MANY BILLIONS

Approved as interim prime minister by Afghan elders, Hamid Karzai (age 44) made a big hit in Washington. The "chicest man on the planet," observed Gucci designer Tom Ford, referring to Karzai's baby sheepskin hat (karkul) and bright green-plus-lavender silk cape (chapan) worn over western suits. Karzai left Washington with $15 million for books, vaccinations and agriculture plus a $50 million line of credit, on top of the $296 million earlier promised by the U.S.

Karzai was a Pashtun, but the Americans permitted Tajiks, a single ethnic minority that dominated the Northern Alliance, to control all the new government's "power" ministries—defense, interior, foreign affairs, intelligence—leaving Pashtuns, the country's largest ethnic group underrepresented and disgruntled.

The Karzai government was nearly broke. Its offices lacked desks, chairs, computers, telephones and often electricity. Outsiders donated millions, but billions were needed. Donors feared anarchy and corruption. Work to rebuild the crucial road from Kabul to Kandahar did not begin until late 2003. Most of the $87 billion supplement for security and development Bush requested for 2003-2004 would go to Iraq, with a few leftovers for Afghanistan.

A LONG SLOG AHEAD,
RUMSFELD CONCEDES

Defense Secretary Rumsfeld maintained that the rout of the Taliban vindi-
cated his reliance on lean, well-financed, high tech operations. Critics said
America should have invaded Afghanistan in force, surrounded al Qaeda,
and eliminated it. Instead the U.S. sent in small numbers of Special Forces,
zapped Taliban bases with smart bombs, paid local warlords to fight on the
ground, and then watched as they let al Qaeda slip across the border into
Pakistan—a haven from which they reentered Afghanistan to harass Karzai
and the Americans.

U.S. combat forces, numbering only 7,000 in early 2000, concentrated in
Kabul and along the Pakistan border. An International Security Assistance
Force deployed mainly around two airports. Dubya, the anti nation-builder,
pledged to train an Afghan national army of 70,000 men, but that would take
time. Meanwhile, many of the warlords defied the new, U.S.-backed government in Kabul and prospered from unlimited poppy cultivation.

In late 2003, Rumsfeld conceded in a memo circulated to his generals
that America faced a long "slog" both in Afghanistan and Iraq. Worries
multiplied that U.S. forces were stretched too thin, even if they did not have
to fight in Korea or some other theater. Indeed, top policy makers were too
concerned with Afghanistan and Iraq to give much attention to Kashmir,
where two of America's friends threatened themselves and humanity with a
nuclear exchange.

"GOD GAVE US BUSH," PENTAGON
INTELLIGENCE CHIEF REVEALS

Only 12% of respondents in nine Islamic states surveyed in 2003 agreed that "Americans respect Arab/Islamic values." Did the majority know what Donald Rumsfeld's Deputy Undersecretary for Intelligence, Army General William G. Boykin, was saying about Christianity and Islam? In 2002-2003, dressed in his U.S. Army regalia, Boykin described for dozens of evangelical Christian groups his own battle with a Somali (Muslim) warlord, saying "I knew that my God was bigger than his God. I knew that my God was a real God and his was an idol." He said that America's enemy is "a spiritual enemy...called Satan." The enemy will only be defeated, "if we come against them in the name of Jesus." On October 21, 2003, when Senator Diane Feinstein demanded that Boykin's boss take "appropriate action" on Boykin, Rumsfeld refused, saying, "We're a free people." *Newsweek* observed that if Boykin kept talking, Osama could give up making videos.

God, for Boykin, is bipartisan. Why is Bush in the White House? Boykin notes that "the majority of Americans did not vote for him." So Bush is "in the White House because God put him there." But God has done the same thing for "Bill Clinton and other presidents."

Perhaps the muddled feelings of the Pentagon's expert on Islam contributed to the muddled approach taken by the Bush administration to Pakistan. Not only did elements in the Pakistan military and intelligence services help to arm and sustain al Qaeda, but Islamabad's top scientists—surely with government approval—sold nuclear weapons know-how to North Korea, Libya, and other countries.

"I don't see many shades of gray in the war and terror. Either you're with us or you're against us. And it's a struggle between good and it's a struggle between evil."

George W. Bush
February 8, 2002

Chapter 13

TO FIGHT EVIL, MUST ONE DO EVIL?

President Bush and his advisers gave little attention to the possibility of a terrorist attack on U.S. soil until September 11, 2001. They ignored the warning and proposals issued in February 2001, by a bipartisan panel led by former U.S. senators Warren B. Rudman and Gary Hart. The panel warned: "The combination of unconventional weapons proliferation with the persistence of international terrorism will end the relative invulnerability of the U.S. homeland to catastrophic attack. A direct attack against American citizens on American soil is likely over the next quarter century. The risk is not only death and destruction but also a demoralization that could undermine U.S. global leadership. In the face of this threat, our nation has no coherent or integrated governmental structures."

The Hart-Rudman commission, composed of high-ranking military and former Cabinet secretaries, called for creation of a Cabinet-level "Homeland Security Agency" to assume responsibility for defending the United States against the increasing likelihood of terrorist attacks. The new agency would take charge of the Federal Emergency Management Agency, Customs Service, Border Patrol and Coast Guard. Guided by the Homeland Security Agency, the National Guard would be "reorganized, properly trained and adequately equipped" to cope with natural disasters and attacks on U.S. targets by weapons of mass destruction. The commission said that the National Guard should be relieved of the responsibility of participating in overseas deployments and concentrate on security at home. The panel also outlined a far-reaching reorganization of the Pentagon, State Department, National Security Council and other agencies, saying that they have become bloated and unfocused. Finally, the report also urged Congress to streamline its own committee structure to keep interference in national security matters at a minimum.

Only after 9/11 the Homeland Security Agency was created in 2002 and its director given cabinet-rank. As of 2004, however, many soft U.S. targets such as chemical plants, nuclear power stations, and ports enjoyed only spotty protection. Many members of the National Guard found themselves not protecting the nation but carrying out a variety of missions in Iraq. The United States remained highly vulnerable to terrorist attacks, even as federal authorities constrained the rights and liberties of U.S. citizens.

THE MAYOR'S PRESENCE,
THE PRESIDENT'S VOICE

The day after 9/11, White House officials said the president would visit New York City "at the first opportunity," but that he did not want to hamper rescue operations in lower Manhattan. Two days after 9/11, Zev Chafets wrote in *The New York Post* that "Bush has yet to find his voice." There were no such questions about Mayor Rudolph Giuliani, said Chafets: "In the face of the worst catastrophe in New York City history, he has been shaken but utterly resolute." Nine days after 9/11, however, the president gave a strong speech, declaring that "we are a country awakened to danger and called to defend freedom" and vowing to "bring our enemies to justice or bring justice to our enemies."

ASK NOT WHAT YOU CAN
DO FOR YOUR COUNTRY....

"Either you are with us, or you are with the terrorists," said President Bush on September 20, 2001. "Freedom and fear are at war," he said. "Be ready," he told the armed forces. "The hour is coming when America will act." But he cautioned that America's enemy "is not our many Muslim friends...our many Arab friends. Our enemy is a radical network of terrorists and every government that supports them."

The president promised a strong campaign to wipe out evil at home as well as abroad. He called for patriotic fervor, but not for sacrifice—not even for higher taxes to pay for damage done or to improve security. His biggest and boldest request went to American consumers: Buy more to get the economy humming. Bush did not urge cutting back on fuel consumption so as to reduce dependence on imported oil. He pressed for additional rounds of tax cuts even though new security outlays were adding to the budget deficit.

DENOUNCING EVIL

Many stalwart politicians took the bold step of denouncing the 9/11 terrorists. They were joined by millions of Americans who purchased and waved more flags. More young men and women inquired about military service, but enlistment rates remained as before. Apart from footballer Pat Tilman (killed in Iraq in 2004), did any stars on a national sports team interrupt their careers, as Red Sox slugger Ted Williams did in World War II and again in the Korean War, when he flew combat missions as a Marine pilot? Or, if they thought America's wars were wrong, did any celebs step forward and say "count me out" as Mohammed Ali did in the Vietnam War?

A PHRASE GEORGE ORWELL
WOULD RELISH

"We're an open society, but we're at war." This was the message President Bush delivered on November 29, 2001, to the annual meeting of U.S. attorneys. America, said GWB, "must not let foreign enemies use the forums of liberty to destroy liberty itself." The Attorney General, meanwhile, used his Orwell-speak to announce the Responsible Cooperators Program. This was a plan to let foreigners extend their stays in the U.S. with three-year "S" visas and possibly ease their way to U.S. citizenship—if they provided "critical and reliable" information to the FBI about terrorists or planned terrorist attacks.

Before Ashcroft announced the Responsible Cooperators Program, law enforcement agencies had already "invited" some 5,000 men to schedule interviews. Most had entered the country in the previous two years and lived

in Arab-American and Islamic communities. Ashcroft's offer looked like a sting operation to trap would-be immigrants, because a Justice Department memo stated that those who volunteered information should be detained on immigration violations if the FBI was interested in them.

The American-Arab Anti-Discrimination Committee noted that the word "cooperator" had an extremely negative connotation in Arabic. The committee could have added that Palestinians regularly executed "cooperators" in Israel's "Occupied Territories."

FORGET OSAMA, LET'S TARGET OREGON!

In November 2001, seeming to have plenty of time and resources available even after 9/11, Mr. Ashcroft ordered government agents to thwart the euthanasia law twice approved by Oregon voters. This was a strange way to express the administration's tilt toward states' rights. In April 2002, U.S. District Judge of Oregon Robert Jones ruled against the Justice Department. The judge asserted that the federal government was trying to usurp the rights of a state when the Justice Department announced it would prosecute doctors who prescribed lethal doses of drugs to terminally ill patients on their request. Not only was Ashcroft attempting to stifle a debate in various states regarding physician-assisted suicide, said Jones, but the Justice Department had also, "with no advance warning...fired the first shot in the battle between the state of Oregon and the federal government." Undaunted and with plenty of resources still available, the Justice Department appealed. It asked the Ninth Circuit Court of Appeals in San Francisco to strike down the statute.

THE FBI TUNES IN TO THE CONFESSIONAL

Many Americans across the political and ideological spectrum questioned legal aspects of the war on terrorism. The N.Y.-based Center for Constitutional Rights challenged the executive order signed by President Bush on November 13, 2001, allowing special military tribunals to try foreigners charged with terrorism. The order seemed to suspend the *writ of habeas corpus*. The American Civil Liberties Union said the White House was purloining the lawmaking role reserved for Congress—a point on which Senator Arlen Specter (R-Penn.) and many Democrats agreed. The Cato Institute objected to the president's November 13th order authorizing officials to detain noncitizens without court approval. The National Association of Criminal Defense Lawyers protested monitoring of some conversations between lawyers and their clients, which it said was like "putting the FBI's ear to the confessional." The president of the Arab-American Institute summed it up: "Military tribunals, secret evidence, no numbers on how many people the government is detaining. We're looking like a Third World country."

COURTS, "NO"; GITMO, "SÍ"

"Military tribunals to try suspects, sanctioning widespread wiretapping and allowing conversations between lawyers and detainees to be monitored—it sounds typical of a country ruled by communists or a military *junta*. But these new measures are being considered by none other than the United States of America." This observation in *New Straits Times* (Kuala Lumpur, Malaysia, December 3, 2001) illustrated how Ashcroft's prosecution of the war on terror struck some foreigners who had for a time admired America's system of justice and civil rights. Malaysia, of course, was no paragon of fair play, but many people there and in other countries edging toward democracy had seen the USA as an example of how justice should and would be carried out.

The detention and treatment of nearly 700 alleged al Qaeda and Taliban members at "Gitmo," the U.S. base at Guantánamo Bay, Cuba, inspired the relatively moderate *Muslim News* (London) to comment: "The lawlessness of the U.S. is a projection of the unsavoury ferocity of the global hyperpower.... Out of the window has gone any regard for the norms of international law and order." In truth, the detention of what the Pentagon calls "illegal combatants" since 2002, indefinitely and with no kind of hearing, probably breaches international law. But Secretary Rumsfeld has said his main concern is to keep bad guys off the streets. However, none of the top al Qaeda leaders captured since 9/11 was ever sent to Guantánamo, according to *Vanity Fair* (January 2004), and the value of the information received from those interrogations at Gitmo was low. In November 2003, the U.S. Supreme Court agreed to hear cases filed by 16 detainees—12 Kuwaitis, two Brits and two Australians—asserting a right to appeal their detentions in U.S. courts. One of the few positive gains from the operation is that Cheney's old friends at Kellogg, Brown & Rent were taking in at least $135 million for building air-conditioned cells and watchtowers ringed by razor wire.

THE NRA TRUMPS THE FBI

"The U.S. will lock people up, but not check on guns," observed *The Gazette* (Montreal) on December 11, 2001, after the U.S. Justice Department forbade the FBI from checking its own records to see if any of the 1,200 or so persons detained after 9/11 had bought guns. FBI agents wanted to use the data on gun purchases already contained in their files, but Ashcroft said no. This would violate the privacy rights of foreigners—including those being detained. A "stupefying contradiction" said *The Gazette*. "In other words, we'll lock you up with no trial, interrogate you with no lawyer present, secretly wiretap your friends and relatives—but heaven forbid we invade your privacy by checking so see whether you've bought any guns during your stay in the United States." "Absurd and unconscionable" said Larry Todd, a California police chief serving on the firearms committee of the International Association of Chiefs of Police.

DUBYA AND ENRON GET A NEARLY FREE RIDE

The president's war on terrorism put Democrats on the defensive. Bush's State of the Union address on January 29, 2002, jolted his approval ratings from 77%—already quite high—to 91% of respondents who thought he would move the country in the right direction. Democrats did not object to the speech's patriotic tone. But House minority leader Richard Gephardt staked out a right for Democrats to develop their own economic policy. Gephardt's eight-minute reply to the president mentioned Enron by name just once as he called for a system of pension benefits "that follows a worker from job to job through life and protects employees from the next Enron." Gephardt called on Congress and the Bush administration to protect workers' pensions "from corporate mismanagement and abuse." He also sought to pressure Bush on money in politics. Gephardt argued that "the nation's largest bankruptcy coupled with a clear example of paid political influence" demonstrated the need to reform campaign finance.

HOMELAND SECURITY @ $25 MILLION = COLOR CODED ALERTS

Tom Ridge, the former Pennsylvania governor catapulted to head the Office of Homeland Security (budget only $25 million but located close to the Oval Office), was in the news in March 2002. He negotiated a new border agree-

ment with Mexico and unveiled a color-coded warning system on threats to public safety (red = severe). But Dubya would not let him testify before the Congressional committees that oversee and finance homeland security operations.

Some Republicans as well as Democrats dismissed Dubya's contention that Ridge, as a presidential advisor, need not appear before Congress. At a House appropriations subcommittee hearing, Representative Ernest Istook

(R-Oklahoma) listed Mr. Ridge's executive functions. They included protecting transportation and food supplies and coordinating border security and responses to terrorist threats. These functions required accountability to Congress, Istook said, and "to deny the testimony of the director of homeland security is to deny the Congress its constitutional role." Similar concerns were voiced by Senators Ted Stevens (R-Alaska) and Richard C. Shelby (R-Alabama), the senior Republicans on the Appropriations and Intelligence committees.

THE BENEFITS OF PRIVATIZATION

Six months after 9/11, the Huffman flight school in Venice, Florida, got notice that student visas had been approved for presumptive skyjackers Mohammed Atta and Marwan Al-Shehhi. What happened? In August 2000, Huffman submitted student visa applications for the two aspiring pilots, one of whom had a business visa and the other a tourist visa. Each man paid $27,300 and completed flight training in January 2001. The INS approved their visas in Summer 2001, but the private contractor in London, Kentucky, hired to do paperwork did not notify Huffman until March 2002. Learning of all this while skimming the front pages, Dubya said he got "plenty hot." But he refused to let Homeland Security Director Tom Ridge appear before a Senate committee to talk about such matters,

for this—horrors!—would mean an intolerable erosion of executive branch power. In August 2001, to ensure a high level of expertise, Dubya appointed as the new INS Commissioner the Senate's former sergeant-at-arms, James W. Ziglar. The INS had about 2000 investigators dealing with millions of persons on temporary visas.

BIG BROTHER VS. WHISTLE-BLOWERS

At first FBI Director Robert S. Mueller, denied that his agency had any advance warning of the 9/11 attacks. On May 30, 2002, however, he conceded that if the FBI had put all the "tidbits of information together" over time, "it's not totally impossible that perhaps we would have gotten lucky...." What provoked this wimpish change of tune? A lawyer in the FBI's Minneapolis office sent a 13-page, heavily footnoted letter to Mueller and several members of Congress, excerpted in *Time* (May 21, 2002).

Coleen Rowley, having dreamed of joining the FBI since the 5th grade, had served 21 years with the agency. The sole breadwinner for six, she hoped her whistle-blowing would not jeopardize her job. Still, she accused Mueller of "a delicate and subtle shading/skewing of facts"—realities that are "omitted, downplayed, glossed over and/or mischaracterized in an effort to avoid or minimize personal and/or institutional embarrassment on the part of the FBI and/or perhaps even for improper political reasons."

Not only did FBI Headquarters (FBIHQ) not link the dots, it ignored or even tried to suppress information about Zacarias Moussaoui, later suspected of being the missing "20th hijacker." Believing flight school student Moussaoui a terrorist threat, the Minneapolis office of the FBI arrested him on August 15, 2001, for overstaying his visa. Within days, French intelligence confirmed that Moussaoui, a French citizen, was affiliated with radical Islamic groups and activities connected to Osama bin Laden. Desperate to search Moussaoui's laptop and his personal effects, the Minneapolis field office asked FBIHQ to approve a request for a criminal search warrant from the U.S. attorney general's office in Minnesota. But FBIHQ was skeptical that a criminal violation had occurred/was occurring. Only after planes had struck the World Trade Center did Minneapolis obtain a search warrant—on the morning of 9/11. Even then, the FBI Supervisory Special Agent (SSA) in Washington tried to prevent Minneapolis from investigating their suspect. Besides its other blunders, FBIHQ did not share relevant information according to Rowley, "HQ personnel never disclosed to the Minneapolis agents that the Phoenix division had, only approximately three weeks earlier, warned

of al Qaeda operatives in flight schools seeking flight training for terrorist purposes!"

Nor did FBIHQ personnel do much to disseminate the information about Moussaoui to other appropriate intelligence/law enforcement authorities. Rowley wrote that, "when, in a desperate 11th hour measure to bypass the FBIHQ roadblock, the Minneapolis Division undertook to directly notify the CIA's Counter Terrorist Center (CTC), FBIHQ personnel actually chastised the Minneapolis agents for making the direct notification without their approval!"

After disclosures that an FBI agent in Phoenix had written a memo in July 2001, asking whether Osama bin Laden was behind the large number of Arab men taking flying lessons in the U.S., Rowley told Mueller, "your statement has changed.[1] The official statement is now to the effect that even if the FBI had followed up on the Phoenix lead to conduct checks of flight schools and the Minneapolis request to search Moussaoui's personal effects and laptop, nothing would have changed and such actions certainly could not have prevented the terrorist attacks and resulting loss of life....Although your conclusion otherwise has to be very reassuring for some in the FBI to hear being repeated so often...your statements demonstrate a rush to judgment to protect the FBI at all costs...."

CENTRALIZED SECURITY OMITS THE
THREE MOST IMPORTANT AGENCIES

How to neutralize Rowley's charges? "Action...camera!" In June 2002, having earlier rejected calls by Democrats to streamline homeland defense, the White House proposed that the Office of Homeland Security become a cabinet-level department to direct and coordinate the security efforts of 22 disparate agencies—from the Coast Guard and FEMA to Customs and the Immigration and Naturalization Service (INS). The clash of cultures, objectives, egos and systems would hardly bolster security for the foreseeable future. Some 75 agencies concerned with national security were left outside the new department's umbrella, including the three most important, the FBI, the CIA, and the National Security Agency (responsible for making and breaking coded messages). Each was protective of turf and budget. Indeed, the new intelligence unit within the new department might add to the cacophony. Developed without consulting the Cabinet or Congress, the size (at least 170,000 employees) and scope of its missions made the new department the most far-reaching restructuring of the federal government since the onset of the Cold War. The department started with a budget of a mere $38 billion, but would surely grow over time.

My country 'tis of thee,
Sweet land of liberty,
Of thee I sing.

From every mountain side,
Let freedom ring!

—*Samuel Francis Smith,* 1831

The Patriot Act already permitted a person's home to be searched without him/her being informed that a search was ever performed or of any surveillance devices that were implanted. But Ashcroft called for a broadening of FBI powers, implying they had been too circumscribed by liberal legalities. Rowley's letter, however, argued that the FBI already had ample powers to investigate, but that FBIHQ was deaf or indifferent to reports from the field. HQ, she implied, lacked not only the coordination to add 2 + 2 but also the "INTEGRITY" (her capitals). She complained that even after FBIHQ knew all the facts described in her letter, "the SSA (Supervisory Special Agent), his unit chief and other involved HQ personnel were allowed to stay in their positions and, what's worse, occupy critical positions in the FBI's SIOC Command Center after September 11th. (The SSA in question actually received a promotion some months afterward!)"

In June 2002, Senator John Edwards suggested that David Frasca, head of the FBI's Radical Fundamentalist Unit (and quite possibly the SSA castigated by Rowley) had misled the Judiciary Committee when he testified in January 2002.

ANOTHER ENEMY COMBATANT?

When U.S. authorities arrested U.S. citizen José Padilla—a.k.a. Abdullah Al Muhajir—at Chicago's O'Hare airport in May 2002, they did not obtain an arrest warrant showing probable cause (such as planning mass murder). They labeled him a "material witness" in an ongoing grand jury investigation of terrorism. In this way they managed to bypass the 5th and 6th amendments and statutes intended to protect the accused. In June, Padilla was transferred from control of the U.S. Department of Justice to a navy brig in South Carolina. President Bush designated Padilla an "enemy combatant." Though not captured in Afghanistan, he was accused of plotting heinous acts of terrorism, particularly the setting off of a "dirty bomb". He was accused of conspiring with members of al Qaeda, using the benefits of his U.S. citizenship. But on December 18, 2003, the 2nd Circuit Court of Appeals said the president did not have the power to detain Padilla as an enemy combatant, and ordered that he be released or transferred to the civilian justice system in 30 days, in which case he could still be held as a material witness.

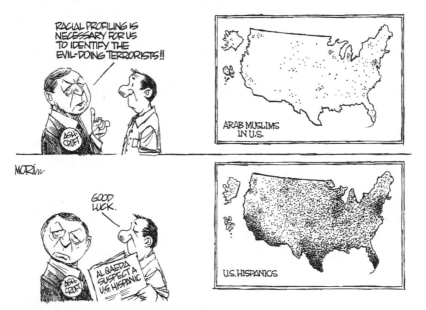

1984 ARRIVES TWO DECADES LATE

Operation TIPS, as unveiled by the Justice Department and the Pentagon in 2002, stood for "Total Information and Prevention System." Everyone's every electronic transaction and communication—from medical prescriptions to e-mails to bank transactions—would be recorded in a centralized data-base. Besides electronic intelligence, TIPS would use human snitches. The Justice Department launched a pilot program in August 2002, involving one million workers in ten cities, but Ashcroft planned a nationwide program giving millions of American truckers, letter carriers, train conductors, ship captains and utility employees a formal way to report suspicious terrorist activity. TIPS would allow these workers, well-positioned to recognize un-usual events, to report suspicious activity. Ordinary souls, not officially part of TIPS, could phone their suspicions and accusations to a toll-free number and be connected directly to TIPS HQ. Its boss was John M. Poindexter, former President Reagan's national security advisor and a convicted felon (convicted of lying to Congress about the Iran-Contra affair).

Troubled by the Big Brother overtones, the government changed the official name to TIA—Terrorist Information Awareness. In July 2003, the Senate blocked spending on aspects of electronic surveillance. The next month, Poindexter resigned after another of his brainstorms, a lottery to highlight likely terrorist attacks, stirred controversy. In 2004, however, the government wanted to color code airplane passengers on the basis of their electronic records.

On July 30, 2003, the American Civil Liberties Union and six Muslim groups brought the first constitutional challenge to the U.S.A. Patriot Act, the sweeping anti-terrorist legislation passed soon after the 9/11 attacks. The suit sought to have Section 215 of the law declared unconstitutional on the grounds that it violates the privacy, due process and free speech rights of Americans. The ACLU chief lawyer said: "There are basically no limits to the amount of information the FBI can get now—library book records, medical records, hotel records, charitable contributions...and it's the secrecy of the whole operation that is really troublesome." The Muslim plaintiffs complained that, because of the secrecy provisions built into the Patriot Act, they had "no way to know with certainty" that the FBI had used its expanded surveillance powers against them. A Muslim group from Ann Arbor maintained that they had been unfairly singled out by the FBI and that some of their number had been imprisoned and deported. The Justice Department replied the Patriot Act closed gaping holes in the government's ability to collect vital information on criminal terrorists.

BE AFRAID...AND DO AS YOU'RE TOLD

The main reason most Americans endorsed President Bush was that he talked and looked like a vigorous defender of U.S. security. Perhaps people were drawn to him when reminded that evil-doers still menaced the homeland. Perhaps orange and red alerts served this purpose. Tom Ridge advised Americans to travel and live as usual, but to report suspicious activity. If nothing happened during the alerts, the Bush team could say its vigilance had paid off.

How often should they cry "Wolf!"? Did it really help homeland security to scare people unless the alarm signaled a need to change daily routines? If the government observed terrorists plotting, why not just keep this intelligence quiet and act to foil the attackers?

The administration nourished a culture of fear. Few Americans would know that the State Department reported one-third fewer international terrorist incidents in 2002 than in 2001—199 down from 355.

In 1933, another president took a different approach. FDR assured Americans that "The only thing we have to fear is fear itself: nameless, unreasoning, unjustified terror…"

> *Let music swell the breeze,*
> *And ring from all the trees*
> *Sweet freedom's song.*
> *Let mortal tongues awake;*
> *Let all that breathe partake;*
> *Let rocks their silence break,*
> *The sound prolong…*
>
> *Long may our land be bright*
> *With freedom's holy light…*

—Samuel Francis Smith, 1831

Chapter 14

WAR: POLITICS BY OTHER MEANS

The Bush plan to attack Iraq ran so contrary to American values and U.S. interests that it led the political counselor of the U.S. Embassy in Greece to resign from the Foreign Service. John B. Kiesling explained to Colin Powell:

> Our fervent pursuit of war with Iraq is driving us to squander the international legitimacy that has been America's most potent weapon of both offense and defense since the days of Woodrow Wilson. We have begun to dismantle the largest and most effective web of international relationships the world has ever known. Our current course will bring instability and danger, not security....
>
> We have not seen such systematic distortion of intelligence, such systematic manipulation of American opinion, since the war in Vietnam. The September 11 tragedy left us stronger than before, rallying around us a vast international coalition to cooperate for the first time in a systematic way against the threat of terrorism....[But] this Administration has chosen to make terrorism a domestic political tool, enlisting a scattered and largely defeated al Qaeda as its bureaucratic ally. We spread disproportionate terror and confusion in the public mind, arbitrarily linking the unrelated problems of terrorism and Iraq. The result, and perhaps the motive, is to justify a vast misallocation of shrinking public wealth to the military and to weaken the safeguards that protect American citizens from the heavy hand of government. September 11 did not do as much damage to the fabric of American society as we seem determined to do to ourselves....We should ask ourselves why we have failed to persuade more of the world that a war with Iraq is necessary. We have over the past two years done too much to assert to our world partners that narrow and mercenary U.S. interests override the cherished values of our partners.... The model of Afghanistan is little comfort to allies wondering on what basis we plan to rebuild the Middle East, and in whose image and interests. Have we indeed become blind, as Russia is blind in Chechnya, as Israel is blind in the Occupied Territories, to our own advice, that overwhelming military power is not the answer to terrorism?[1]

THE PASSIONATE QUEST OF
PASSIONATE CONSERVATIVES

Some of Bush's advisers had wanted to polish off Saddam Hussein some ten years earlier. When 9/11 came along, they made their move. They generated a rationale for invading a country that had not attacked America.

It appeared that George Senior tried to curb his son's lust to blast Saddam. His two major assistants on foreign affairs, James Baker and Brent Scowcroft, published op-eds urging restraint, as did Henry Kissinger. A rift emerged between moderate Republicans and passionate conservatives close to Dubya—Donald Rumsfeld, Dick Cheney, Paul Wolfowitz, Richard Perle and perhaps Condoleezza Rice. The passionates dispatched former CIA Director R. James Woolsey to Europe in September 2001, in quest of evidence that might link Saddam Hussein to the 9/11 attacks.[2]

Deputy Secretary of Defense
Dr. Paul Wolfowitz aimed to
democratize the Middle East.

A HEDGED ESTIMATE TWISTED
INTO A RATIONALE FOR WAR

The president and his aides gave two reasons to carry out a regime change in Iraq: First, that Iraq actively supported the 9/11 attacks and second, that Iraq was both buying and building weapons of mass destruction (WMD)—biological, chemical and nuclear. Since Saddam Hussein might transfer WMD to al Qaeda or other terrorists, the U.S. should not just watch and wait. It

The Pentagon's man for Baghdad, Dr. Ahmed Chalabi, assured Americans that Iraqis would greet U.S. troops as liberators, but Washington disowned him in May 2004.

needed to pre-empt any attack. Neither assertion was true—as many analysts said at the time. Many Americans later blamed the CIA for false reports when they should have blamed the White House for distorting the evidence.

The National Intelligence Estimate (NEI) delivered to the White House in October 2002, claimed only that Saddam's regime was continuing to pursue WMD. "If left unchecked, it probably will have a nuclear weapon during this decade....How quickly Iraq will obtain its first nuclear weapon depends on when it acquires sufficient weapons-grade fissile material." A dissenting view from the State Department intelligence unit (INR) said it was impossible "to predict when Iraq could acquire a nuclear device or weapon." It noted that the U.S. Department of Energy believed the aluminum tubes Iraq tried to buy abroad were not suitable for use in gas centrifuges to enrich uranium. The NEI seemed to accept reports that Iraq was seeking to acquire uranium ore in Niger, Somalia and the Congo, but INR regarded these claims as "highly dubious." [3]

The NEI said that Baghdad had "begun renewed production" of chemical weapons, but "its capability probably is more limited now than it was at the time of the Gulf War." The NEI judged that "Iraq has some lethal and incapacitating BW [biological weapons] agents and is capable of quickly producing and weaponizing a variety of such agents...." Within three to six months of October 2002, Iraq could probably produce as much BW agent as it possessed before the Gulf War.

The NEI continued: "Baghdad for now appears to be drawing a line short of conducting terrorist attacks with conventional or CBW against the United States, fearing that exposure of Iraqi involvement would provide Washington a stronger cause for making war." But a revenge attack with BW was deemed possible, though chemical weapons were more likely than biological to be used on the battlefield.

The NEI warned that Baghdad's unmanned aerial vehicles (UAVs) could threaten Iraq's neighbors, U.S. forces in the Persian Gulf and even the U.S. homeland. But the director of U.S. Air Force reconnaissance programs did not agree that Iraq was developing UAVs primarily as delivery platforms for CBW agents. He believed that "the small size of Iraq's new UAV strongly suggests a primary role of reconnaissance...." (Subsequent up-close inspection made these "UAVs" look more like jury-rigged high school workshop experiments.)

The NEI expressed "low confidence in our ability to assess when Saddam would use WMD—whether preemptively or to disrupt U.S. war preparations or to stall a U.S. military advance. The most likely scenario was that Saddam would try to use WMD if "he irretrievably had lost control of the military and security situation...."

Obliquely discounting a Saddam-Osama nexus, the NEI stated that "Saddam, if sufficiently desperate, might decide that only an organization such as al Qaeda" could mount a CBW attack against the U.S. "In such circumstances, he might decide that the extreme step of assisting the Islamist terrorists in conducting a CBW attack against the United States would be his last chance to exact vengeance by taking a large number of victims with him."

President Bush conceded after the war that there was no evidence Saddam had ever helped al Qaeda. Most experts agreed that the secular government in Baghdad and the devout Osama despised each other. Theirs was a true clash of cultures—worldly materialists vs. religious purists.

The NEI apparently said nothing about the victims of Saddam's torture chambers—later given as a reason to overthrow him. As for Saddam's gassing his own people, Washington said nothing about it at the time, even though Cheney was in Baghdad as it happened!

On February 3, 2003, speaking as though the NEI did not exist, Secretary of State Colin Powell cited Iraq's WMD as grounds for war. He told the UN Security Council that "every statement I make today is backed up by sources, solid sources. These are not assertions. What we are giving you are facts and conclusions based on solid intelligence." A year later, his reputation and that of his government lay in tatters.

The recently resigned chief U.S. weapons inspector David Kay stated in January-February 2004, that U.S. and some foreign intelligence agencies had been wrong. There probably had been no stocks of WMD in Iraq before the U.S. invasion and it appeared unlikely that any would be found. The Kay report led Congress to demand an investigation into why American intelligence had been so wrong. But Kay's assertions were untrue and served merely to let Dubya and his intimate circle off the hook. The NEI quoted here shows that U.S. intelligence had been carefully modulated. The consensus was far less alarmist than what Bush, Rumsfeld, Rice and Powell had presented to the world in 2002 and early 2003. Indeed, Powell's own intelligence bureau, INR and the head of Air Force surveillance were even more cautious than the consensus. Yes, there had been major gaps in U.S. intelligence, but its estimates did not justify the rush to war mobilized by the White House. Speaking at Georgetown University on February 5, 2004, CIA Director George Tenet implied that the White House had transformed a carefully hedged estimate into an unqualified rationale for pre-emptive attack.

BLAIR JOINS THE MINISTRY OF UNTRUTH

After some hesitation, Tony Blair lined up squarely with Bush. The British government warned that Iraq could mount an attack on the UK with WMD in just 45 minutes. Two independent think-tanks in London disagreed. The

International Institute for Strategic Studies and Jane's publishers estimated that Iraq could probably develop a nuclear weapon in a few years, but only *if* it somehow acquired a sufficient quantity of fissionable material. Both think-tanks concurred that Iraq had been developing chemical and biological weapons, but opined that these were not practical battlefield weapons, especially since Iraq possessed very few missiles that could even reach to Israel. Many in the British establishment later said the Blair team had "sexed up" the known facts. A British judge concluded that the PM had told no direct lies about Iraq's WMD. But outsiders judged that Blair and his aides had distorted the evidence no less than the Bush team. In time, both Blair and Bush would be asked to answer for the ways that their exaggerations led to great harm to individuals who had served their country with great dedication and skill—among them, the UK scientist David Kelly, who slashed his wrists (BBC News, July 19, 2003) and CIA operative Valerie Plame (see p. 196).

A DANGEROUS DOCTRINE CONFUSES LONG-TERM WITH IMMEDIATE THREATS

The White House called for a "pre-emptive" strike but what it really meant was "preventive war." The distinction is crucial. A pre-emptive strike is launched to disarm a foe preparing to attack in the very near future—perhaps in hours or days. Thus, in 1967 Israel destroyed Egyptian planes while still on the ground. By contrast, a preventive war moves against an enemy before

its military buildup can shift the balance of power—a matter of months or years. For example, Berlin and Tokyo started World War II before their foes' re-armament could catch up with head starts by Germany and Japan.

As the cartoon suggests, a U.S. attack on Iraq could lead other players to justify their wars as "pre-emptive." Either India or Pakistan might say it intended to pre-empt the other's attack.

WHAT'S THE RUSH?

Many wondered: What's the rush to deal with Saddam? His wrongdoings were no worse in 2002 than before. There was nothing about any of his weapons making it imperative to attack him immediately. North Korea and Iran posed more imminent nuclear threats.

The only pressing date on the horizon was November 2002, when elections would decide which party controlled the U.S. Senate and House of Representatives. Other U.S. presidents may have carried out small-scale interventions, as in Grenada or Haiti, to deflect attention from problems elsewhere. But those invasions were pocket change compared to what the Bush team contemplated. To attack Iraq and destroy the regime there would present immense, unfathomable dangers and difficulties. The more bombs, the more mistakes. Recall the U.S. bomb that demolished a bunker in Baghdad sheltering civilians in 1991.

WAR AS THE
CONTINUATION OF POLITICS

He stole the election two years before. In 2002, it seemed he was out to steal a second by a stratagem likely to cost many lives and much treasure. On September 25, Senator Tom Daschle detailed the evidence. Republican pollsters, Vice President Dick Cheney, and the president himself assured the Republican faithful that they had a winning issue for the November 2002, elections if they focused political debate on war. Who could complain about unemployment, dwindling pensions or the environment if the U.S. were struggling to rid the world of monsters? Even though Democrats pushed through most of the country's military buildups in the 20th century (except for that of the 1980s), many people saw Democrats as "soft on defense."

Questions arose: How could an administration allergic to "nation-building" dream it could democratize a large and traditionally Islamic country with deep internal cleavages? Did America have a General Douglas MacArthur ready and waiting to disarm, democratize and de-cartel a vanquished Iraq? Had Americans mastered the small-scale challenges of Lebanon, Somalia, Haiti, Bosnia, Kosovo and Macedonia? Did Iraqi politicians in exile show much ability to compromise and cooperate?

WHY SO TOUGH ON BAGHDAD
BUT NOT PYONGYANG?

U.S. diplomats at the United Nations championed the need for unfettered inspection of Iraq's suspected weapons facilities. But when Baghdad agreed to "unconditional inspection" (excluding presidential palaces), the White House raised the bar. It demanded "disarmament"—not just inspection. The Americans gave Saddam no positive incentive to cooperate—no hope that, even if Iraq were found purged of WMD, UN sanctions would be removed.

Critics wondered why the U.S. negotiated grudgingly with North Korea but not Iraq. Was Kim Jong-Il, who watched his people starve by the million, any better than Saddam? Was it that Iraq had oil and North Korea had only weapons?

Meanwhile, Washington did little to bolster the existing treaties banning biological and chemical weapons. U.S. diplomats scuttled efforts to tighten enforcement of the Biological Weapons Convention (initiated by President Nixon) because the measures proposed could permit foreigners a closer look at U.S. industries. Also, Washington was slow to pay its bills for chemical weapons monitoring and never called for a "challenge inspection" of suspected violators such as Iran.

LET THEM HATE US SO
LONG AS THEY FEAR US

Diktat. This German word summed up the problem. Washington's efforts to dictate to others reminded some Germans of Adolf Hitler and heralded a new chapter in Dubya's manual on how to lose friends. Chancellor Gerhard Schröeder's defiance of Washington on Iraq helped his "red-green" coalition win Germany's September 2002, parliamentary elections. When Paris and Berlin balked at following America into war, Rumsfeld wrote them off as "old Europe." Writing from Athens, U.S. Foreign Service Diplomat John Kiesling asked Colin Powell if the U.S. motto had become Caligula's *oderint dum metuant* ["let them hate us so long as they fear us"]. Kiesling observed: "After the shambles of post-war Iraq joins the shambles in Grozny and Ramallah, it will be a brave foreigner who forms ranks with Micronesia to follow where we lead….The loyalty of many of our friends is impressive, a tribute to American moral capital built up over a century. But our closest allies are persuaded less that war is justified than that it would be perilous to allow the U.S. to drift into complete solipsism….Why does our President condone the swaggering and contemptuous approach to our friends and allies this Administration is fostering, including among its most senior officials?"

DISSENT = UNPATRIOTIC ?

Dubya charged that Senate Democrats were putting partisan interests above national security when they balked at permitting him to hire and fire Homeland Security employees at will. In response, on September 25, 2002, Senator Daschle demanded that the president apologize to Dan Inouye and all the other Democratic senators who had risked their lives in battle for the country.

AN UNHOLY ALLIANCE

The Russians were more inclined than the Germans or French to go along with the United States on Iraq. Moscow insisted on a free hand to continue its futile war in Chechnya in exchange for permitting the United States to risk disaster in Iraq. On September 11, 2002, anniversary of the World Trade Center collapse, President Putin echoed Bush's warnings to the Taliban and Iraq. Putin threatened preemptive strikes on Georgian territory unless Tbilisi cracked down on Chechen rebels, who had recently shot down three Russian helicopters.

Caveat emptor: Since 1999, the Russians had lost nearly 5,000 soldiers;

the Chechnyans, more than twice that number. If Russia could not subdue Chechnyans after nearly a decade, how difficult would it be for the United States to subdue Iraq? Russian policies had Islamicized Chechnya. Would Washington do the same in Iraq? Meanwhile, Americans and Russians met in Houston to discuss ways to reap joint benefits from Iraqi oil.

AMERICA DECEIVED BY WISHFUL
THINKING AND HUBRIS

In early May 2003, less than two months after the invasion of Iraq began, President Bush flew onto an aircraft carrier and announced an end to major combat in Iraq. When resistance to U.S. occupation emerged, Dubya smirked: "Bring 'em on!" For the rest of 2003 and into 2004, hostile forces mounted almost daily attacks on U.S. soldiers and anyone who seemed to collaborate with them—Iraqi police, mullahs, even the UN and the International Committee of the Red Cross. In 2003, the UN and many humanitarian agencies pulled out most of their personnel.

This kind of chaos had been predicted by State Department and other experts on the Arab world before the war began, but the Pentagon and White House did not listen to any views that challenged their own wishful-thinking. Instead they listened to exiles with major axes to grind such as Ahmad

Chalabi, a mathematics professor and banker (convicted of fraud in Jordan). Chalabi had not been in Baghdad since the late 1950s, but he had founded the Iraqi National Congress in 1992, an umbrella group for Iraqi opposition groups in exile. Terrible planning as well as bumbling execution made the extremely difficult job of rebuilding Iraq even harder.

WHITE HOUSE TREASON

The Bush team sank to a new low when challenged about 16 words in the President's 2003 State of the Union address: "The British government has learned that Saddam Hussein recently sought significant quantities of uranium from Africa." In 2002, when the British reported that Iraq had looked for "yellowcake" in Niger, the CIA asked retired Ambassador James C. Wilson IV, to investigate. Wilson knew Iraq as well as Africa—he was the last high-ranking U.S. official to talk with Saddam Hussein in 1990. Having traveled to Niger to check out the story, he told the CIA it was a fabrication.

　　Shocked to see a myth presented as fact by Dubya—a pretense to attack Iraq—Wilson warned that if Condoleezza Rice did not correct the record, he would. Stonewalled, he published "What I Didn't Find in Africa" (*The New York Times*, July 6, 2003). Who would now take the blame? CIA Director

George Tenet said he should not have permitted the misstatement to enter the president's speech. Next, Dr. Rice conceded that her NSC should have looked more carefully at the text. Finally, the president said that he was responsible for everything in the speech.

The dagger in the back came on July 14, 2003: Columnist Robert Novak wrote that Wilson's investigation was a "low level" CIA project and that agency higher-ups deemed its conclusion "less than definitive." Novak added that 'two senior administration officials" told him Wilson got the job only because his wife, Valerie Plame, an "agency operative on weapons of mass destruction," had suggested him to her bosses.

What a strange way to protect the president and get back at Wilson—destroy a valued asset, sacrifice her career and risk the lives of everyone abroad who had dealt with her! And at a time when everyone said the CIA needed more "human resources"! The Intelligence Identities Protection Act makes it a federal crime, punishable by up to 10 years in prison, to leak the name of an undercover agent. Dubya's father told a CIA audience on April 16, 1999: "I have nothing but contempt and anger for those who betray the trust by exposing the name of our sources. They are…the most insidious of traitors." His son, however, seemed undisturbed. On October 7, 2003, the President of the United States observed that "this is a town full of people who like to leak information. And I don't know if we're going to find out the senior administration official [singular]."

Not just Democrats but even CIA Director Tenet demanded an independent investigation. However, the President handed over the inquiry to the Justice Department, where the Attorney General promised a professional investigation. But could Mr. Ashcroft sever his umbilical cord to the White House, where Dubya's chief strategist was a prime suspect? One journalist had told Wilson: "I just got off the phone with Karl Rove. He says your wife is fair game." Six journalists heard about Plame but only one, Novak, saw fit to expose her. After some delay, Ashcroft turned over supervision of the investigation to his deputy, who brought in a respected outsider to run it. Still, an in-house job might be biased. Wilson tells his version in *The Politics of Truth: Inside the Lies that Led to War and Betrayed My Wife's C.I.A. Identity, A Diplomat's Memoir* (2004).

DISINFORMED AND DELUDED

A survey in August 2003, showed that 69% of Americans believed Saddam Hussein was involved in the 9/11/01 attacks—an opinion artfully cultivated by Dick Cheney and other White House officials. In September 2003, however, President Bush said there was no evidence for this view.

TV left most Americans disinformed. Surveys conducted by the University of Maryland in September 2003, revealed that 48% of Americans believed that links between Iraq and al Qaeda had been found; 22%, that WMD had been discovered in Iraq; and 29%, that world public opinion favored

America's invasion of Iraq. Overall, 60% had swallowed one or more of these untruths. Among the Americans with just one of these misperceptions, 55% supported the war—a share that rose to 86% of respondents mired in all three misperceptions.

The leading channel for disinformation was Fox News. Some 80% of Fox viewers accepted one or more of the three false propositions, compared to just 23% of PBS viewers. CBS and ABC performed slightly better than Fox, while only 55% of ABC and CNN watchers were led astray. Even Americans who depended mainly on print media were confused: 47% accepted at least one of the three big lies.

War takes a toll on the home front. It came right to the door of St. Joseph's church in a three-block long town in New Mexico, where everyone knew that the pastor, Jesuit priest John Dear, opposed the Iraq war. In November 2003, the local National Guard unit learned it would soon depart for Iraq. The next day at 6 a.m. the usual desert stillness shook to the sound of 75 soldiers jogging down Main Street chanting, "Swing your guns from left to right, we can kill those guys all right." An hour later they stood outside Dear's front door screaming, "Kill! Kill! Kill!" Dear stepped out and told them to go home, resign from the guard, and practice nonviolence. "New Mexico," the priest observed, "is the poorest state in the U.S. It is also number one in military spending and number one in nuclear weapons (Los Alamos, Sandia). It is the most militarized, the most in need of disarmament, the most in need of nonviolence. It is the first place the Pentagon goes to recruit poor youth into the empire's army." (Dear was profiled in *The New York Times*, October 4, 2001, as he ministered to victims of 9/11. See also: www.fatherjohndear.org).

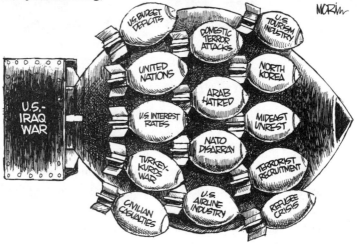

CLUSTER BOMB

A BALANCE SHEET: SADDAM
GONE, BUT AT WHAT PRICE?

Consonant with Machiavelli's advice to make bold, sudden moves, Dubya showed up unannounced for Thanksgiving dinner to cheer some U.S. troops in Iraq. As 2003 passed into 2004, the Bush team could take satisfaction that Saddam and his entourage had been removed from power, but they were left with a score of deficits:

- No WMDs found—deepening doubts about Dubya's credibility.
- No links found between Iraq and al Qaeda.
- No obvious reduction in terrorist threats to the U.S.
- NATO weakened, with France and Germany more determined to set up a European force independent of U.S. influence.
- The already ballooning federal deficit aggravated by at least $200 billion in extra costs for Iraq in 2003-2004 (omitting subsequent bills for veterans' benefits).
- No imminent prospect of large-scale oil production in Iraq.
- No smooth consolidation of democracy in Iraq.
- Little near-term hope in Iraq for streets safe from criminals and terrorists
- One tactical error after another by the U.S. administrators in Iraq (for example, dismissing 400,000 armed soldiers without pay).
- Weakening of the U.S. armed forces, stretched too thin (one-third of all combat troops were in Iraq at the end of 2003, tired and disgruntled; many regulars and reservists disinclined to reenlist).
- Disruption of family and work as reservists serve long tours abroad.
- Reduced U.S. ability and willingness to take on North Korea.
- No evident increase in democracy within other Middle Eastern countries.
- No evident gain in U.S. capacity to understand Iraq or other parts of the Islamic world (*cf.* General Boykin).
- Deepening and broadening of hatred toward the U.S. in most of the Islamic world.
- Failure of U.S. public diplomacy efforts to "sell" the U.S. to the Muslim world lacked focus, direction, money and policies that might elicit a positive response. Some Republicans who voted in 1998 to fold the U.S. Information Agency into the State Deptartment and cut its personnel by 40% admit they made a mistake.
- No gains for Israel, the Palestinians, or their peace process.
- Reduced pressure on Beijing and Moscow to respect human rights as the U.S. asks them for support or acquiescence in its Iraq policy.
  - No easy handoff of Iraq's administration to the UN
  - Weakening of the UN and other institutions of global governance by U.S. unilateralism.

Instead of honoring its war dead killed in its optional war, the Bush administration flew in coffins returning from Iraq so they arrived in the dark. The White House tried to keep photographers away, pre-empting displays that might arouse a somewhat blasé public. But some photographers managed to document the mounting tragedy. For a collection see: www.thememoryhole.org.

Still other horrifying images from Iraq appeared in *The New Yorker* and its Web site in May 2004, as Seymour M. Hersh reported in "Chain of Command" on the abuse and torture of Iraqi prisoners in U.S.-run prisons. What many saw as a "public relations Pearl Harbor" gutted American claims to unusual virtue. Readers of this book would not be surprised, however, to find more evidence that the Bush administration was callous toward the incarcerated, even if many were innocent; indifferent to law, due process, and world opinion; inclined to believe that might makes right; and confident that its denials and obfuscations could persuade the public that black is white. On May 10, 2004, Dubya reassured Americans that the Secretary of Defense was doing a "superb job." Rush Limbaugh and his callers decided that stacking naked Iraqis, bruised and bloodied, on top of each other or pulling them on a leash was akin to a college prank. "Axis-of-evil" expositor David Frum was reported to believe that Americans were not too upset by the prison photos, because they could not forget what Iraqis and other Arabs had done to Americans.

PENTAGON ACCOUNTABILITY

If America's goals had been to remove a tyrant from power and assure that no Iraqi WMD were pointed at America or its friends, the mission had been accomplished. Probably it was time to withdraw U.S. forces from Iraq before they or Iraqis suffered any more from their presence.

Meanwhile, Halliburton prospered. Its oil field contracts were worth about $77 million in May; $1.5 billion in October; and $2.2 billion in December 2003. Also, Iran and Libya said they would forgo nuclear arms (at least for the present) and North Korea showed a renewed willingness to discuss its nuclear programs.

"I try to go for longer runs, but it's tough around here at the White House on the outdoor track. It's sad that I can't run longer. It's one of the saddest things about the presidency."

George W. Bush
August 21, 2002

Chapter 15

PAY-OFFS: THE WORST PRESIDENCY IN U.S. HISTORY?

George W. Bush entered the White House with the United States on top of the world. No other president began his term with the country so strong—not just in material power but also in the influence that comes from respect. Soon, however, Dubya and team eviscerated these assets. Has any other leader in U.S. history done so much so quickly to harm America at home and globally?

Dubya stands out among U.S. presidents for having done so much harm in nearly every field where he has left a mark—in foreign as well as in domestic affairs. In each case the Bush team won some immediate gain for its narrow interests but caused lasting damage to the country and sometimes to the world. Let us count the ways.[1]

MORALITY

Do what is needed to succeed, Machiavelli advised the prince, and nobody will care if you offend morality and law. This is how Dubya built his wealth and power. The man's character revealed itself in Texas long before he took the country by coup in 2000. No president in the past century had grown up basking in such political and economic privilege, but none had wasted his assets so thoroughly—at school and later. No other president carried the psychological traits and burdens of a recovered alcoholic, including arrest for DUI (driving under the influence) at age 30. None, having found a way to evade active military service, avoided even his quite limited reserve duties so often and for so long.

No president had such a record of failed and shady business dealings sustained by family cronies. His failure to report insider trading was judged by SEC officials to have violated the law, but with George the Elder still president, he was not prosecuted.

As if harking to Machiavelli's advice on executions, Governor Bush helped his state lead the nation in administering capital punishment. Nonchalant about others' deaths, Dubya expressed confidence that justice was always done on his watch.

No other politician did so much to permit—virtually encourage—pollution as GWB when, as governor, he extended deregulation of Texas.

GWB was one of just four candidates elected to the U.S. presidency despite losing the popular vote—the first since Benjamin Harrison in 1889. He was the only one helped by dubious election procedures supervised by his own brother (governor of Florida) and his local campaign manager (who—conflict of interests!—was also Florida's secretary of state), and by an unprecedented intrusion into state politics by a majority of Supreme Court judges, some of whom had deep ties to the Bush dynasty.

No other administration—not just the president but also several members of his inner circle—relied so heavily on financial support from scam artists, con men, suspected or even convicted felons.[2] The vice president's old firm, Halliburton, continued to pay him for past services even as it expanded its revenues in tandem with the U.S. military—from the Philippines to Iraq to Guantánamo.[3] Even as Halliburton shareholders benefited from U.S. largesse, the company avoided paying U.S. taxes by incorporating in tax havens from Bermuda to Vanuatu.[4]

Cheney had the gall to send out Christmas cards in 2003 dominated by the question:

> And if a sparrow cannot fall to the ground without His notice,
> Is it probable that an empire can rise without His aid?[5]

Was the inference that not just America's military reach but Halliburton's wealth should be attributed to Almighty? Cheney's audacity outstripped Tartuffe's!

To go along with such doings, Americans would have to be either fools or knaves—blind to the Bush team's shady dealings or anxious to emulate them. The president coached Americans to be either dumb or wicked. The president's down-home, plain-speakin' style, combined with his out-front religiosity, encouraged confidence in his moral authority.[6] Nearly half the voters in 2000 chose a man with whom they would enjoy a baseball game, even though the vast majority deemed Al Gore the more knowledgeable and experienced candidate. Even as a child, George W. could get people to laugh. He loafed at sports and at schoolwork, but he made people comfortable. He grew up a con man—inveigling investors to plow money into his oil digs, helping arrangements to cook the books at Harken Energy, persuading town fathers to give him a baseball stadium.

"Shrub" restored to Washington many who had been involved in Enron

or other shady operations. With much to hide, Dubya's people sought to keep the wraps on corporate corruption in America. President U.S. Grant, by comparison, found many rotten apples in his barrels, but he was more deceived than deceiving.[7] Following its "cover-up" strategy, the Bush team refused even to take part in international cooperation to crack down on tax havens. It winked at corporate tax fraud thought to cost honest taxpayers $350 billion a year.

Did Americans wind up with the government they deserved? Yes and no. But most voters did not cast their ballots for Bush. They were cheated by a state administration that disenfranchised thousands of Florida's eligible voters and a Supreme Court majority that intervened to throw the election.

SPIRIT AND THE NATIONAL AGENDA

President George W. Bush did not offer a New Deal, Fair Deal, New Frontier or Great Society—not even a "return to normalcy" or opposition to an "evil empire." His father, though lacking a "vision thing," gave humanity hope for a New World Order. George W. emphasized the negative—not the positive. Instead of encouraging Americans to "ask what you can do for your country," he bemused and titillated them with what they might get, starting with tax cuts. Even after 9/11, the president's idea of exercising America's freedoms was to spend and consume.

To be sure, GWB did espouse laws called "Clean Skies," "Healthy Forests" and "No Child Left Behind," but did so with such evident hypocrisy that his slogans dishonored the ideal (e.g., clean skies). The 43rd president offered no vision-setting agenda except to get richer. Perceiving that this agenda could bolster their wealth, America's plutocrats and kleptocrats forked out thousands in campaign donations, confident their return would run to millions.

This kind of vision brought out the worst in Americans and contributed to deficits at all levels—federal and state budgets, trade and personal (as bankruptcies became more common than divorce).

GLAUCON'S RING AT WORK

Most previous presidents championed openness as a prerequisite for democracy. They saw that societal fitness in all realms requires feedback from informed participants. Not so Dubya and company. Seeking the blinding effects of Glaucon's magic ring, the Bush team labored to mask its actions—past, present and future. Not only did GWB hide his own paper trail as governor but also those of his father's vice presidency. He rebuffed efforts to find out who shaped Dick Cheney's energy plan. When Enron's false accounts were revealed and the firm bellied-up, Bush tried to obscure his ties with the firm and its long-time CEO—his lead source for campaign funding over the years. The Bush White House tried to cloak its dubious dealings in other realms—from 9/11 to ABM test reliability to the public demolition of CIA operative Valeric Plame.

George W. became another "Teflon president." Like Ronald Reagan, many people found it hard to see through him no matter what he did—especially after 9/11. What was good for the current president, however, augured ill for the republic.

PAY-OFFS FOR PASSIONATE CONSERVATIVES

Bushonomics used voodoo chants to mask kleptomania. The Bushites quickly converted a huge budget surplus into a series of escalating federal deficits extending into the future. In January 2004, the Congressional Budget Office predicted that the federal budget deficit would approach half a trillion dollars that year—nearly 5% of gross domestic product—and that accumulated deficits in the next decade would total nearly $2 to 3 trillion. If Congress made tax cuts permanent, as President Bush demanded, total deficits in the next decade would probably run much higher. The White House engaged in what *The New York Times* on January 25, 2004, termed "economic malpractice." Perhaps Dubya's people suffered from "denial"—an inability to face unpleasant facts. More plausibly, they and other rentiers just wanted their bottom lines to increase, no matter what. At least one-third of the deficit resulted from waves of tax cuts, mainly for the rich but falsely advertised as serving the common good. At first Bush manipulated the numbers to make it appear that the budget surpluses would be preserved; then, that they would soon be recovered; finally, that they did not matter.[8] Federal Reserve Chairman Alan Greenspan, who probably knew better, could have raised his voice to check the malpractice but chose not to rock Dubya's boat.

Bush pleased the military-industrial complex by upping military spending by many billions. By 2004, U.S. defense outlays exceeded those of all other industrialized countries combined. Pressed to grant prescription drug relief for seniors, the administration used a private route that guaranteed maximum profits for drug makers even though this added another huge burden to the federal budget.

Dubya's defenders correctly noted that he came to office just as the business cycle turned downward. But GWB did little to prime the pump. The country lost many more jobs than were created on his watch—a feat not achieved since Herbert Hoover. Maybe big gains at the top would be OK if wealth had trickled down, but this did not happen. Bush's policies taxed the richest 1% less and transferred some but not all the burden to other Americans.[9] Some of the burden was left for a later generation to shoulder. A good deal for the few at the top proved to be a raw deal for most Americans—not just for today's taxpayers but for later generations! Passionate conservatives showed no concern for intergenerational equity, i.e., the ideal of passing on a life at least as good as that they had inherited.

In January 2004, America's federal budget deficit and trade imbalance led the International Monetary Fund to warn that they jeopardized not just America's economic health but also the world's. The Bush White House praised the theory of free trade but offered no helping hand or even "compassion" to the textile workers, phone operators and computer programmers whose jobs were "outsourced" to Mexico, India and elsewhere.[10]

Societal fitness also hinges on trust. But who could trust this administration or its cronies? A president who promised to unify the country polarized it instead. The long-term well-being of an economy also requires faith that hard work and thrift will be rewarded. But the example set by Dubya resembled less the diligent heroes described by Horatio Alger and more the Ivanushkas who get their way in Russian folk tales by deceit or good fortune.[11] Indeed, several commentators argued that "Horatio Alger" had died in America because Bush and his crew made it so hard for anyone to pull him (or her) self up by their own bootstraps.

WASTE NOT, WANT NOT?

Confronted with the costs of heavy reliance on fossil fuels, the administration told Americans: "Carry on!" On Dubya's watch the nation's reliance on imported fuel increased, with no turn-around in sight. Yes, he tried to open more of America to oil and gas exploration, but his biggest efforts went to securing strong U.S. influence over the oil resources of Kazakstan, Azerbaijan, Iraq, Siberia, Nigeria, Ecuador and Indonesia. This orientation set the stage for confrontations not only with local protestors but also with other oil-hungry giants such as China and Japan. Reliance on fossil fuels endangered the global environment by raising the level of greenhouse gases. It also symbolized a decline in America's capacity for innovation. Dubya's

team assumed that a mere update of century-old technologies would suffice for the 21st century rather than searching hard for new ways to travel, heat, lubricate and fertilize. Cheney said conservation might be a virtue but could not serve as the basis for policy. In 2002, the fuel economy of the average new vehicle sold in the U.S. fell to 20.4 miles a gallon, its lowest point in 22 years, according to the EPA, based on data that *excluded* the largest SUVs and pickup trucks, not regulated by fuel economy rules.[12]

Myopic as well as selfish, the Bush team sought to free the energy business from oversight by government or the scrutiny of environmental and consumer whistle-blowers. It tried to prevent limits to the price gouging by Enron and other energy traders gang-raping California. Its hands-off orientation set the stage for an East Coast blackout when a Bush client in northern Ohio failed to modernize its plants and transmission grid.[13]

THE DEMOCRACY MONEY CAN BUY

In 2000, candidate George W. quickly attracted so many fat cats ("Pioneers") to his cause that he rejected government funds in the primaries, a feat he would repeat in 2004. As president, George W. rewarded his backers—not with a night or two in the White House, but with open sesames to previously protected public goods.

Dubya's major foe in the 2000 primaries, Senator John McCain, worked for years to reduce the role of "soft money" in elections. Despite White House obstruction, McCain's finance reform law was enacted. When a court upheld the bill, both parties invented other ways to tap interested sponsors.

As the 2004 election year began, Dubya had already amassed over $130 million for his campaign chest. In the 2000 elections, no major financial services were among Bush's top ten supporters. By January 2004, however, his top donors included Merrill Lynch and five other brokerages—visibly enraptured by Bush's opposition to dividend and capital gains taxes and his support for private investment accounts to be included in the Social Security system, schemes that would bring billions in annual fees and commissions to Wall Street firms.[14] Perhaps Dubya's wand could also help deflect the class-action suits brought by investors against many of these firms, such as Credit Suisse First Boston and Goldman Sachs, accused of misleading or cheating their own clients.[15] As of September 2003, Goldman Sachs had donated $343 million to Bush, $111 million to John Kerry, and $80 million to Joseph Lieberman.[16]

Knowing that money can talk, Republicans overthrew the usual timetables in California and Texas and tried to do so elsewhere. In 2003, they stoked up a campaign to recall California's recently re-elected governor, Gray Davis, and replace him with Arnold Schwarzenegger. In 2003, they managed to re-redistrict Texas to assure six or seven more Republican seats in the House of Representatives, though redistricting had already taken place on the basis of the year 2000 census and by Texas custom, would not occur again for ten years.[17] Every major newspaper in Texas said the new map was unnecessary and unfair, but a three-man federal court said re-redistricting did not violate Texas law (after which the attorney who argued the case for re-redistricting billed the state for $736,000). A Colorado court, however, blocked a similar effort there on the basis of federal law.

ADMINISTRATIVE EFFICIENCY

Bush ran a tight ship. Most of his appointees spoke from the same script, except for the guerrilla warfare between Powell and Rumsfeld, and the president's tendency to cut off the EPA at the knees if it got too green. The Bush team's hard-line zealotry cost it a party-line majority in the Senate when Jim Jeffords bolted from Republican ranks in 2001. Helped by the aftermath of 9/11, however, Republicans regained both houses of Congress in 2002.

Revelations that the president spoke falsehoods about Niger, Iraq's WMD and other matters stirred some controversy between the CIA and the White House. Was the CIA incompetent or had it been bludgeoned to produce a script the White House demanded?

Divisions also arose within Republican ranks as conservative conservatives (better late than never) caught on to the likely dimensions of the federal
deficit in years to come. In January 2004, for example, they were shocked
when the White House raised its estimate of the recently enacted drug benefit for seniors from $400 billion over the next decade to $540 billion. Some
Republicans wanted to starve "the beast"—their term for the welfare state.
Few faced up to the impact of the tax cuts—which were responsible for at
least one-third and perhaps one-half of the overall deficit.

The most outspoken of Bush's initial team proved to be former Treasury
Secretary Paul O'Neill, who, after he was fired, accused the president of
many lapses.[18]

AMERICA'S THREAT TO THE BIOSPHERE

Bush is the least "green" modern president. Reverence for nature was out;
exploitation was in. The greatest Republican president of the 20th century,
Theodore Roosevelt, campaigned for wild places and against big trusts that
harmed the public interest. President George W. moved the other way. He
enjoyed an occasional bird hunt but nearly every day connived to remove
barriers so big companies could rip into wild places to extract oil, coal,
minerals and timber. Deregulation is the Bush mantra—unprotect rather
than protect. Bush invited snowmobilers to fume the snows and air of Yellowstone, and found one court willing to approve a "compromise" likely to
devastate a world treasure.

Is environmental preservation a frill? Ask those who dwell near Superfund waste sites whose cleanup funds were nearly exhausted in 2004, or people who live downwind from power plants who suffer asthma and worse. Ask those who feel they must drink bottled water and avoid fish laced with mercury. Ask rangers at Yellowstone's gate wearing respirators when hundreds of snowmobilers chug by.

Dubya torpedoed the Kyoto protocol and any other serious measure to reduce carbon emissions. A threat to the entire biosphere, the U.S. produces at least a quarter of the world's greenhouse gases and sets a model for other polluters to emulate. For now, Americans can endure and pay for the bizarre weather patterns they help to induce. For Bangladeshis and others, however, global warming spells death. Drowning humans may cry out, but coral reefs beneath the warming waters utter no sound as they shrivel and bleach. Extinct species are silent.

The White House nearly ignored international conflicts over water and other resources. It promised much but did little to cope with AIDS and other diseases ravaging Africa and other regions. In January 2003, Bush stirred African hopes by pledging $15 billion to combat AIDS over five years, including $10 billion in "new money," but then the administration requested only $1.9 billion in its 2004 budget request to Congress, much of it derived from cuts in other international health-care programs. In January 2004, the administration asked for $2.5 billion for bilateral programs but—allergic to multilateral endeavors—cut its donation to the UN Global Fund to Fight AIDS, Malaria and Tuberculosis from $550 million to $200 million. While niggardly about AIDS, the administration took a strong stand against international standards of truth in advertising the dangers of tobacco and fat-soaked foods à la Golden Arches. Long live free choice!—except when the issue was mind food.

MIND CONTROL, DRILL AND KILL

True, President Bush did not himself own any TV networks, as did Italian Prime Minister Silvio Burlusconi. But Fox News served the purpose. Fox, plus a pack of radio hipsters, hyped the president's policies for mass audiences. These arrangements were facilitated by positioning Colin Powell's son, Michael, as the chairman of the Federal Communications Commission.

No 20th century president talked less grammatically or appeared more ignorant of America and the world than did George W. That he and his football coach pal from Houston could sell a vast educational reform to Congress beggars the imagination. But they did. America's pupils faced a routine of high-stakes tests that, if they succeeded, might produce dutiful robots.

By 2004, the president's signature education act had put more than a quarter of the nation's public schools on academic probation because they failed to make "adequate yearly progress." If they failed for a second consecutive year, they would be obliged to provide transportation for pupils to transfer to higher-scoring schools; for a third year, tutoring. But the No Child law was so poorly funded that some school districts revolted. The president of the Virginia Board of Education said the law's formula for determining adequate yearly progress was "irrational and lacks common sense." The law penalized a state that was already a leader. But it also placed impossible demands on schools in poor areas where everything was in deficit—hope, motivation, family support and tax base.

From chaos, private gain. The Bush dynasty profited as brother Neil exploited the "standards" hysteria to sell teaching machines. On the bright side, as of 2004, the Bush brothers had not yet tried to export to other states the textbook censorship system deployed in Texas.

The Bush team also harmed education indirectly. By pushing more and more fiscal obligations onto states but without the money to support them, Washington forced state and local governments to cut resources for education and other services. Pressured to balance their budgets, states cut vital social programs. Some half million children were among the 1.6 million Americans who lost health coverage in the Bush years. They included 160,000 Texas children, where some of the biggest cuts took place.[19] More people might go without health coverage in 2004, as states faced a collective budget deficit of nearly $50 billion.

An underlying problem, of course, is drugs. But was it really useful to spend huge sums—$1.3 billion on Plan Colombia—to extirpate foreign supplies?[20] Why not use the money to reduce demand? Why not build a salubrious recreation and education center in each troubled neighborhood? What if the funds used to incarcerate one criminal—on average, some $30,000 per year—were used to buy him or her a first-rate education and/or anti-drug therapy? Jailing one man in New York City ran to $50,000 a year—nearly enough to pay for two years at Columbia University! The bottom-line for Bush was really "Leave no millionaire behind." While the No Child Left Behind reforms gave a few more dollars to pupils and teachers in inner-city schools, Bush's serious largesse showed up in tax cuts. A study sponsored by the Children's Defense Fund showed that the best-off 1% of U.S. taxpayers would receive 52% of the cuts scheduled for the decade beginning in 2002— an average of $342,000 each. Most Americans would receive a tax break closer to $500 each—most of it in 2002. For people too poor to pay taxes, a tax break would mean nothing. Also, they would remain uninsured—their health needs met, if at all, in the emergency rooms of city hospitals. In time, children born during Dubya's reign would inherit part of a $2 to 3 trillion national debt expected by 2012, the result of a plan to enrich the rich at the cost of everybody else.

THE FIRST AMENDMENT

Far more than any other president, George W. cut away at the separation between state and church. One tool was faith-based initiatives; another, school vouchers. Dubya's ideal judge, Antonin Scalia, lamented the tendency of democracy to question the divine authority of government. Justice Scalia lined up with fundamentalists who urge revolution if their views on law and morality are not adopted in government policy.

Bowing to Christian Conservatives, the administration restricted abortion in the U.S. and cut off financial assistance to UN family planning and health programs.

As to the rest of the Bill of Rights, Dubya permitted his Attorney General to shrink virtually every right except the alleged right of private citizens to carry guns. Skirting the Constitutional requirement for Senate approval, the president appointed two ultra conservatives to federal appeals courts while Congress was in recess.[21]

HOW TO LOSE FRIENDS AND INSPIRE ENEMIES

In October 2000, Candidate George called for an America "humble" in world affairs. "If we're an arrogant nation, they'll resent us. If we're a humble nation, but strong, they'll welcome us." On becoming president, however, he put the country on an arrogant course of imperial expansion not seen since the time of Spanish-American War. Compare Bush's strut across the global stage with the course recommended by FDR in 1933:

> In the field of world policy I would dedicate this Nation to the policy of the good neighbor—the neighbor who resolutely respects himself and, because he does so, respects the rights of others—the neighbor who respects his obligations and respects the sanctity of his agreements in and with a world of neighbors.

"Just-say-no" became the watchword as the Bush team shredded U.S. ties with traditional allies by its ham-handed unilateralism.[22] Washington warned Europeans not to go it alone militarily even as Bush threatened to leave them holding the bag in the Balkans and elsewhere. Bush raised steel tariffs even as he called for "free trade." Having alienated much of Europe, Bush did nothing to help flailing Japanese governments.

In 2001, Dubya insulted both Beijing and Moscow. He cast China as a peer rival America had to contain; Russia, as a nonentity. After 9/11, however, Bush embraced Chinese and Russian leaders as dear buddies—never mind how they treated Uighurs and Tibetans, Chechens and Georgians. The reborn Christian in the White House and his State Department did almost nothing to protest the treatment of Catholics and Protestants by Putin's Orthodox Christian regime. As for Uzbekistan, never mind how the government treated its own Uzbeks—especially those trying to practice an Islam not aligned with the dictatorship.

The Bush administration did little to contain the possible spread of "loose nukes" stolen or purchased from Russia's poorly guarded collections of weapons and fissionable materials. Its policies encouraged a buildup of U.S. and Chinese armed forces for an eventual collision.

It winked at severe human rights abuses in Saudi Arabia, the Philippines and elsewhere as long as foreign partners acquiesced in or helped America's way of fighting terrorism.

So hostile was the Bush White House to the rule of law that it purported to "un-sign" the statute of the International Criminal Court, which had been signed but not ratified in the Clinton years. So puffed up with self-righteousness were the White House and Congressional Republicans that they agreed to punish any country that adhered to the ICC without specifically excluding U.S. citizens as potential defendants. Washington proceeded to cut military aid to many countries that refused to sign these agreements, even though they presumably served U.S. objectives. The U.S. had become a "bungling bully," said Great Britain's major business paper. "Bullying is reprehensible in any circumstances," observed the *Financial Times* on July 3, 2003, "But simultaneously shooting oneself in the foot looks like incompetence."

Disdainful of treaties, the president tore up the antiballistic missile pact with Russia without Congressional approval—provoking some thirty congressmen to sue the president for violating the Constitution and precedent. Other suits by former Pentagon insiders accused the Pentagon of doling out missile defense contracts without bidding. The General Accounting Office warned that the technologies being deployed for a national missile defence (NMD) were not proven effective—not alone and certainly not together. Even though 9/11 showed that terrorists could employ many tools against America other than ICBMs, Dubya began to deploy a NMD with no assurance it would work and no idea of its ultimate cost.

Dubya lumped three very different countries into an imaginary "axis of evil." This phrase acted like a self-fulfilling prophecy. Saddam Hussein was obdurate; Iran and North Korea, less so. The Bush team did little to strengthen moderates within Iran and, in 2001, broke off negotiations that promised to curb North Korea's missile as well as its nuclear potential. Dubya's people used neither sticks nor carrots to influence Pyongyang. Was this because, if North Korea's nuclear-missile threat subsided, there would be no point to building a missile shield? [23]

The Middle East remained the Achilles Heel of U.S. foreign policy. Nearly everything that Yasser Arafat and Ariel Sharon said or did served to intensify the Palestinian-Israeli conflict. But Bush did little to intervene and, by tolerating the Israeli wall and other actions, spiked Muslim anger toward the United States.

Gathering its muscle, the U.S. could do its thing and call on others to follow. Both the president and Dr. Rice complained they could not understand the resentment stirred by U.S. unilateralism. "Like most Americans," said Dubya, "I just can't believe it. Because I know how good we are." They could not imagine that others would doubt the purity of U.S. motives.[24]

HAS THE WAR ON TERRORISM
IMPROVED AMERICAN SECURITY?

The Bush team seemed not to anticipate 9/11, but it acted afterwards to restore public confidence fairly quickly. George W. Bush followed Machiavelli's injunction to exploit war and foreign affairs to consolidate power at home. He waved the banner of anti-terrorism to silence nearly all questions about his administration's behavior.

The administration disposed of the Taliban regime and Saddam Hussein in short order. But major problems remained. The Taliban was marginal-

ized, but Osama and al Qaeda still threatened the world. Saddam was in jail, but anti-American forces terrorized Iraq. The number of Muslims—men and women—willing to die fighting the U.S. and Israel grew. Anti-American sentiment in the Islamic world increased—thanks in part to U.S. "occupation" of Iraq and to U.S. toleration of brutal Israeli policies toward Palestinians.

Every misstep taken by L. Paul Bremmer III, the U.S. administrator in Iraq, screamed to high heaven: Neither he nor most of the Americans seeking to govern Iraq knew the languages and cultures of the Islamic world. Yes, U.S. technology could readily tap more phones but America had few specialists able to decipher the messages and communicate with people in the region.

Those whom Americans took into custody in Afghanistan and Iraq were labeled "unlawful combatants" and denied the protections provided to "prisoners of war." The Bush legal team tried to minimize any role for civil or even military courts in dealing with accused terrorists and "unlawful combatants."

The Department of Homeland Security looked like a Rube Goldberg contraption. From some perspectives it tried to do too much; from other perspectives, too little. While trying to coordinate nearly two dozen agencies, each with a distinct mission, Homeland Security Chief Tom Ridge had no control over scores of other agencies concerned with security—including the Big Three: the FBI, the CIA, and the National Security Agency.

Security controls at airports were tightened, but those at ports and road

crossings looked very spotty. Several years after 9/11, the protection of America's nuclear, chemical and other industrial installations was left mainly to their owners.

The color-coded alerts announced intermittently after 9/11 reminded Americans of peril and encouraged them to stick with their leader. Outsiders could not know if the alerts helped fend off dangers. Security at New Year's and other public celebrations came to entail the whir of helicopters overhead, arrays of anti-aircraft guns, the deployment of snipers. As Teresa Simon-Noble wrote early in 2004: "Generalized anxiety, a fear of terrorism and the possibility of terrorist attacks cloud the mind of many thinking people, obscuring the realities of what George W. Bush's presidency has inflicted on people living on fixed incomes who suddenly find that their check…is no longer sufficient to meet all their living expenses." [25]

The administration's mentality was revealed in its TIPS plan to enlist 4% of the citizenry to keep tabs on the other 96%. The plan was quickly quashed when even the Christian Right protested. By early 2004, however, the Department of Homeland Security was investigating how to color code the security risk posed by every airplane passenger on the basis of his or her credit card and other computerized records. Would they obtain the electronic records of Yemenis and Saudis as well as Brits and Ohioans? Would airlines conduct their own checks or funnel e-data to Washington? Would Big Brother do the work itself or farm it out to private firms such as Torch Concepts in Huntsville, Alabama—a Pentagon contractor that obtained computerized passenger data from JetBlue Airways in February 2004, in violation of the 1974 Privacy Act? [26]

BALANCE SHEET: PERFORMANCE
WITHIN THE CONTEXT OF THE TIMES

To evaluate a presidency we must consider the severity of the problems it faced and the strength of its assets. The Bush team entered office with unparalleled assets relative to the challenges it faced at home and abroad. The problems confronting the Bush team in 2001 were serious but modest—almost trivial—compared to those that faced, say, James Madison, James Buchanan, Abraham Lincoln, Franklin D. Roosevelt or Harry S. Truman. On the other hand, the assets that Dubya inherited were many times greater than those enjoyed by all his predecessors except Bill Clinton. Frittering away enormous hard and soft power, Dubya and his people improved nothing and made most things far worse:

• The ultra rich got richer but the economy lost jobs over four years.
• The federal budget went from black to deep red. State governments also plunged into red ink. The trade imbalance yawned. Personal debt ballooned.
• The quality of American democracy and civil society declined. Having widened the rift between "two Americas," one for the ultra rich and one for everybody else, the Bush team derided complaints about this polarization as "class warfare."
• The ranks of Americans without health insurance increased. Health care costs rose to 15% of GDP (in tandem with profit margins at drug companies)
• For retirement savings, the Bush team threw caution to the winds and urged partial privatization of Social Security.
• Passionate conservative policies deepened and embittered partisan alignments. Tension between religious fundamentalists and other Americans became sharper.
• The quality of America's education system probably declined.
• Environmental protection programs went into a tailspin.
• The credibility of the U.S. government collapsed at home and abroad, tainting not just the Bush administration but dragging down all Americans.
• America's influence and image in the world collapsed as many—perhaps most—peoples and governments disliked U.S. hegemony and did what they could to weaken it.

Why? Americans permitted a cabal of selfish, narrow-minded Machiavellians to impose their agenda on America and the world. Proud and mighty, White House planners sought to transform the world—relying heavily on force. Soon, however, they managed to make the U.S. the most reviled nation on earth, to gut its economy, to strangle its schools; and to punish a suffering planet with more carbon emissions. Were their ears open, the president and his advisers might hear Goethe's chorus lament:

> *Alas! Alas!*
> *You have shattered*
> *The beautiful world*
> *With a mighty fist:*
> *It falls, it is scattered—*
> *Destroyed by a demigod!*

We carry
Its wreckage over into the Void
And cry
For beauty undone. [27]

Goethe's spirits did not surrender hope. They hoped the world would be rebuilt—a new way of life, constructed with a clear mind and fresh songs.[28] Faust himself was saved because he labored to this end. He was saved because he worked for others and for posterity—not for himself. He relished the moment only for what it meant to future generations.

Freedom and life are earned only by those
Who conquer them each day anew. [29]

NOTES

Introduction

[1] See Howard Raiffa et al., *Negotiation Analysis: The Science and Art of Collaborative Decision Making* (Cambridge, Ma.: Harvard University Press, 2002) and earlier work by Thomas C. Schelling and Robert Axelrod.

[2] This is the basic conclusion of scholars from many disciplines working on complexity science at the Santa Fe Institute. See Stuart A. Kauffman, *At Home in the Universe: The Search for the Laws of Self-Organization and Complexity* (New York: Oxford University Press, 1995).

[3] Walter C. Clemens, Jr., *America and the World, 1898-2025: Achievements, Failures, Alternative Futures* (New York: Palgrave, 2000).

[4] Walter C. Clemens, Jr., *Dynamics of International Relations: Conflict and Mutual Gain in an Era of Global Interdependence*, 2d ed. (Lanham, Md.: Rowman & Littlefield, 2004).

[5] See the essays on individual presidents including GWB in *The American Presidency*, eds. Alan Brinkley and Davis Dyer (Boston: Houghton Mifflin, 2004).

[6] Kevin Phillips, *American Dynasty: Aristocracy, Fortune, and the Politics of Deceit in the House of Bush* (New York: Viking, 2004).

[7] Maureen Dowd recalls her friend's tale in "The Age of Acquiescence," *The New York Times*, June 26, 2002, p. A23.

Chapter 1

[1] Kevin Phillips, *American Dynasty: Aristocracy, Fortune, and the Politics of Deceit in the House of Bush* (New York: Viking, 2004).

[2] The price of politicking had gone up. Back in 1972, Richard Nixon took in $61 million compared to $40 million for George McGovern, while in 1968 Nixon got by with $25 million versus $12 million for Hubert Humphrey.

[3] In May 1971, Bush requested a six-month transfer to an inactive postal reserve unit in Alabama so he could work in the campaign of a Republican senate candidate. The transfer request was denied by the National Guard Bureau headquarters, but Bush moved to Alabama and stayed there. In August 1972, he was summarily suspended from flying duties. There is speculation that substance abuse played a role. A scanned copy of the memo confirming Bush's suspension from the Air National Guard for "failure to accomplish annual medical examination" can be viewed at: http://daily.misleader.org/ctt.asp?u=2097444&l=15660.

[4] Greg Palast, *The Best Democracy Money Can Buy* (New York: Penguin, 2003), pp. 11-81.

[5] Of course the situation was truly complex. Apologists for all sides fell short of perfect legal

reasoning. See Richard A. Posner, *Public Intellectuals: A Study of Decline* (Cambridge, Ma.: Harvard University Press, 2003).

[6] *The New York Times*, June 29, 2002, p. 17. For background, see David G. Winter's *Personality: Analysis and Interpretation of Lives* (New York: McGraw-Hill, 1995).

Chapter 2

[1] In 2000, Texas had no property tax, no individual income tax, and no corporate income tax. (*Per capita* taxes paid to the state in Texas in 2000 were $1,315—half what they were in California.) Dick Cheney's Wyoming (like three other states) was double zero—no individual or corporate income taxes. Even brother Jeb's Florida had corporate though no individual income taxes. Texas was the only triple zero on taxes in the Union. Individual home owners, however, paid substantial local taxes. The state's tax system left Texas without sufficient funds to meet the state's basic needs, according to the nonpartisan Center for Public Policy Priorities. It called for a state income tax as a more adequate and more equitable solution to funding shortfalls. The U.S. Census Bureau Web site has tax statistics on every state.

[2] A "kleptocrat nation" is "a body of people ruled by thieves...a government characterized by the practice of transferring money and power from the many to the few...[and] a ruling class of moneyed elites that usurps liberty, justice, sovereignty, and other, democratic rights from the people." Jim Hightower, *Thieves in High Places: They've Stolen Our Country—And It's Time To Take It Back* (New York: Viking, 2004).

[3] House Minority Leader Richard Gephardt (D-Mo) said the numbers showed that the recently enacted tax cuts had "obliterated record surpluses and jeopardized virtually every other priority of the American people." But Rep. Jim Nussle (R-Iowa), chair of the House Budget Committee, countered that the tax cuts had laid the basis for economic recovery. "Now," Nussle said, "we have to control Washington's voracious appetite for spending."

[4] The paradoxes of American opinion were brought home to me by a conversation in 2002 with a 60-year-old Boston taxi driver who was reading two big books—one on John Adams and another on Abigail. When he learned I was en route to Montreal to explain Bush policies at the University of Quebec, he was dumbfounded: "What's to explain?" said the driver. "Everybody loves him—here and everywhere." Trying to reach the solar plexus, I asked the driver whether Bush's tax policies had not hurt him and me. "It's only right," he replied, "that rich people get bigger tax cuts, because they have paid most of the taxes." I asked if he ever read *The New York Times*. He replied with an epithet and waved in my face the voice of truth—the tabloid *Boston Herald*.

[5] Paul Krugman, "The Tax-Cut Con," *New York Times Magazine*, September 14, 2003. An economist at Princeton, Krugman earlier taught at M.I.T. and Stanford. Krugman first noticed mendacity in the Bush administration's presentation of economic projections and then found that it extended into other domains. For collected essays, see Paul Krugman, *The Great Unraveling: Losing Our Way in the New Century* (New York; W. W. Norton, 2003).

Chapter 3

[1] Howard Dean placed some of his papers as governor of Vermont off limits unless the state

attorney general made them public. Dean said he did this to respect the privacy of individuals who had written to him, for example, on gay marriage. Many Democrats regarded Dean's position as slouching into the ways of the other side.

[2] Enron documents obtained by the Foundation for Taxpayer and Consumer Rights suggested that far more was at stake. If Governor Gray Davis were recalled and the groper became governor, Schwarzenegger was to settle California's claim against Enron for pennies on the dollar—most of the state's $9 billion claim down the tubes. For details, see: www. consumerwatchdog.org/utlities and www.gregpalast.com.

[3] Letter dated May 6, 2002, from FERC investigator Donald G. Gelinas to Enron counsel James Behrends, IV, Esq.; for a bibliography on the collapse of Enron and legal proceedings, see: http://www.llrx.com/features/enron.htm.

[4] By 2001, outsiders had plenty of info about Ken Lay and Enron and their involvement in Bush politics. See for example, *Mother Jones*, May 5, 2001.

[5] On these cases and the Enron links of Alberto Gonzalez, a White House counsel, Secretary of Commerce Don Evans, and former head of the Christian Coalition Ralph Reed, see the Public Citizen Web site: www.citizen.org.

Chapter 4

[1] Matthew Miller observed in *The San Diego Union-Tribune* on April 20, 2002, that the feds would now match only the first $250 of the $2000 hard money contribution allowed to individuals—a 50% cut from the $250 previously geared to a maximum donation of $1000. This arrangement lowered the cost of refusing funds. While Democrats with relatively little hard money clout would husband their funds and wait for the next tranche, "the hard-money king George Bush will be airing whatever 'morning in America' ads Karl Rove dreams up." The Democrats' weakness in attracting hard money had been offset by Bill Clinton's ability to haul in soft money (remember the Lincoln bedroom?), but any role for soft money was now severely restricted.

[2] Justice Scalia added that "the use of corporate wealth…to speak to the electorate is unlikely to 'distort' elections—especially if disclosure requirements tell the people where the speech is coming from," while political favors done as a *quid pro quo* would violate criminal law. For links to the text of the "Bipartisan Campaign Reform Act of 2002" and its legislative history, the court filings of McConnell and the NRA, plus news articles covering the bill's passage, the president's signing, and the challenges are at: http://www.law.stanford.edu/library/campaignfinance/.

[3] David Frum and Richard Perle, *An End to Evil: How to Win the War on Terror* (New York: Random House, 2003).

Chapter 5

[1] On January 11, 2002, EPA Ombudsman Robert J. Martin filed a conflict of interest lawsuit in U.S. District Court against his boss, Ms. Whitman. He charged she had helped Citigroup to evade most of the charges it should have paid for a nuclear waste Superfund cleanup in

Colorado. Whitman's own public financial reports showed that she and her husband held $100,000 to $250,000 in Citigroup stock. Moreover, Citigroup was a major investor in her husband's venture capital fund. Christie responded by transferring the longtime EPA ombudsman to a corner in the EPA Inspector-General's office, and changed the locks on his files (see his resignation letter of April 22, 2002). What did all this cost the public (apart from the disgrace of being subjected to an administration completely obtuse to conflicts of interest)? At least $14 million. The Colorado cleanup would cost between $22 and $100 million, but Christie got Citigroup's obligations limited to $7.2 million. Another EPA investigator said that if "Whitman doesn't back down on this, we may as well kiss representative government goodbye. Because it means that a top government official can rule in cases that directly benefit her financially, get called on it, tell her accusers to get lost, and get away with it."

In 2003, after Whitman resigned, the EPA thumbed its nose at a federal court ruling (League of Wilderness Defenders v. Forsgren) that the agency must protect lakes, streams, and wells by requiring that pesticide applications be subject to Clean Water Act permits. The EPA refused to compel the U.S. Forest Service to seek a permit before spraying pesticide into U.S. waters. In September 2003, the EPA also announced that fire retardants could be dumped into streams and wetlands without a Clean Air Act permit.

[2] Some observers believed it was time for Congress to simplify the regulatory maze while protecting the nation's health. The 1970 Clean Air Act had not been significantly updated since 1990.

[3] For more chilling tales, see the National Resources Defense Council's "The Bush Record" at: www.nrdc.org.

Chapter 6

[1] Board member Mary Ellen Berlanga warned her colleagues on the State Board of Education that if no books were approved for Advanced Placement courses, students would suffer and might even sue the state. She saw a disconnect between board members' votes against environmental textbooks and the board's insistence that textbooks uphold the free enterprise system. The board could itself support the enterprise of small publishers that followed the procedures to get their books onto the state's "conforming" list, and yet the committee initially voted to reject all but one textbook—giving a monopoly to one company. She noted that board members often endorsed freedom of speech and yet wanted to censor textbooks that do not agree with their philosophy.

Mrs. Berlanga also asked the board not to censor history books and to give high school students an opportunity to study all sides of an issue. One of five Democrats on a board with ten Republicans, she apparently found reason to affirm that she was proud to be an American and that she supported both freedom of speech and the free enterprise system. She indicated her support of adding the LeBel textbook to the conforming list, but objected to a procedure that required last minute rewriting.

For motions and discussions by Mrs. Berlaga and other board members on November 9, 2001, see: http://www.tea.state.tx.us/sboe/minutes/sboe/2001/0111min.html

For an appeal to the board on November 8, 2001 to reject an environmental text that did not respect the values taught in families, see:
http://www.cse.org/informed/issues_template.php?issue_id=748

For an analysis of banned and challenged books in Texas in 2000-2001 by the American Civil Liberties Union, see: http://www.aclutx.org/pubed/bannedbooks/01banned.htm

For an open letter by 136 University of Texas at Austin professors, mostly scientists, to the

Texas Board of Education in 2003, see:
http://www.txscience.org/files/schafersman-oct3-comments.htm
   The signatories said they viewed "with dismay the unnecessary controversy that has arisen over the selection of textbooks for use in high schools in Texas....Students should have full exposure to contemporary evolutionary theory from which there is no scientifically credible dissent nor is there any empirical evidence that would make such dissent plausible."

[2] Writing on NCLB in the journal for professional educators, *Phi Delta Kappan* (April 25, 2003), William J. Mathis reported that for Texas, assuming it kept its basic skills test, the additional cost would be $7 billion. In 2003, New Hampshire received an average of $77 in new federal money for each of 220,000 students, while the obligations of the NCLB law would cost $575 per student. New Hampshire received $17 million in new money from Washington for new obligations of $126.5 million.

[3] Both Texas and North Carolina had high-stakes testing and their students posted huge increases in math and reading on the NAEP in the 1990s. These apparent gains were achieved in part by exempting greater numbers of special education and limited English proficient students. Thus, North Carolina's composite score in 4th grade math increased by 20 points from 1992 to 2000, compared to a national improvement of only 8 points. But North Carolina excluded 4% of its LEP and IEP students in 1992 and 13% of its LEP and IEP students in 2000. Meanwhile, the nation's exclusion rate decreased from 8% to 7% over the same time period. See Audrey Amrein-Beardsley and David C. Berliner in *Education Policy Analysis Archives*, March 28, 2002 and August 4, 2003. http://epaa.asu.edu/epaa/v10n18.

[4] Neil's previous role in the savings and loan debacle cost taxpayers more than $1 billion. Saved from jail (while Poppy was still president), Neil was banned from doing business again as a banker. So he ventured into IT.

[5] Neil's family values suffered during his travels. Despite Neil's Secret Service escort, beautiful women kept knocking on his doors in Asia and, his doors open to the world, he let them in. Vile stories reached Neil's wife in Texas, prompting a messy divorce. Neil offered Sharon $1,000 a month to shut up—a nice offer from one who had to get by on $800,000 in 2000. His American girlfriend, however, ignored the fuss.

Chapter 9

[1] In 2002, the CIA revealed—and Pyongyang confirmed—that North Korea had built a second nuclear complex, beyond reach of the 1994 agreement. But Pyongyang averred that the U.S. and its partners had not upheld their side of the accord. Six years after the framework agreement, the two nuclear reactors it pledged were nowhere close to completion. See Walter C. Clemens, Jr., "Peace in Korea? Lessons from Cold War Détentes," *Journal of East Asian Affairs*, 17, 2 (Fall/Winter 2003), pp. 258-290.

Chapter 10

[1] But the Bush team tried to establish a firm base for its oil interests in Azerbaijan and Kazakstan, where Russia also had oil interests. Thus, Washington pushed Chevron and other western oil companies to bypass Russia by building a pipeline to carry Kazak and Azeri oil from Azerbaijan past Armenia to Georgia and then across the Black Sea to the Turkish port

of Ceyhan. The Bush team ignored the ugly sides of the Azeri and Kazak dictatorships just as it did the Russian and Chinese.

[2] Addressing an EU summit in Brussels on November 11, 2002, Bush's friend the ex-KGB agent declared: "If you want to become a complete Islamic radical, and are ready to undergo circumcision, then I invite you to Moscow. We're a multidenominational country. We have specialists in this question as well. I will recommend that he carry out the operation in such a way that after it nothing else will grow." Though Putin's comments were softened by the interpreter in Belgium, they were later published accurately in Russian newspapers, evoking no comment.

[3] Kaspirov in an op-ed for *The Wall Street Journal*, September 18, 2003.

[4] Still, the FSB may have overstepped in February 2004, when one of the few Russians who dared challenge Putin in the March presidential election reported the security services had drugged him for five days. Gore in 2000, his critics said, did not need to be drugged.

Chapter 11

[1] Both were said to be "Straussians," followers of the political theorist Leo Strauss, a secular Jew who, worried the west was flabby in dealing with Hitler and Stalin, advised his students to use esoteric language while pursuing higher goals. However there seem to be few hidden messages in Perle's book with David Frum, *An End to Evil: How to Win the War on Terror* (New York: Random House, 2003).

Chapter 12

[1] See reports of the United States Commission on National Security/21st Century (the "Hart-Rudman Commission") in 1999-2001 and warnings by FBI field offices dating from the late 1990s, cited by Coleen Rowley in her letter to the FBI director, summarized in the next chapter.

[2] John F. Burns, "Pakistanis say bin Laden may be dead of disease," *The New York Times*, January 19, 2002.

[3] Patrick E. Tyler, "Fearing harm, bin Laden kin fled from US," *The New York Times*, September 30, 2001.

[4] For more such questions and the reports that provoke them, see: www.the-movement.com.

[5] See William Langewiesche, "The Crash of Egypt Air 990," *Atlantic Monthly*, November 2001.

[6] See: www.therightchristians.org/archives.

[7] See below, Chapter 14.

[8] To appreciate the dangers posed by madrassas, U.S. officials did not need to know Arabic, Farsi, or Dari. The 2001 Nobel Prize winner in literature, V.S. Naipaul, depicted these schools

in his *Among the Believers: An Islamic Journey* (1981) and *Beyond Belief: Incursions Among the Converted Peoples* (1998).

Chapter 13

[1] In 1998, the FBI's chief pilot in Oklahoma City speculated that the Middle Eastern men taking flight training in Oklahoma might be planning terrorist activity. His report was entitled "Weapons of Mass Destruction," but its importance was labeled "routine" at FBIHG.

Chapter 14

[1] *The New York Times*, February 27, 2003 and *The New York Review of Books*, April 10, 2003.

[2] For the mood and some of the arguments, see Bob Woodward, *Bush at War* (New York: Simon & Schuseter, 2002), Chapters 4 and 5.

[3] Declassified excerpts, including the dissenting views cited here, were released by the White House and placed in the *Congressional Record*, July 21, 2003, pp. E1545-E1546 and on July 23, 2003, page E1567.

Chapter 15

[1] Presidents can be graded by what they did for the country, at home and abroad, or merely by what they achieved, given their own personal and political objectives. Either way, we have to consider how well they used the resources available relative to the challenges they faced. This chapter reviews the Bush record using the yardsticks employed by C-SPAN when it asks historians to rate the presidents since Washington and in my own surveys of experts asked to evaluate U.S. achievements and failures at home and abroad. For C-SPAN, see: http://www.americanpresidents.org/survey/historians/; for my surveys, see Walter C. Clemens, Jr., *America and the World, 1898-2025: Achievements, Failures, Alternative Futures* (New York: Palgrave, 2000).

[2] In January 2004, hoping that Enron's chief financial officer would spill the beans on Ken Lay, prosecutors sold him a mere ten-year prison sentence as opposed to the twenty or thirty his numerous felonies warranted. Dubya's father and mother, as noted in Chapter 1, hired themselves out to Rev. Moon after he left prison.

[3] While Pentagon auditors scrutinized a number of Halliburton services, including the cleanliness of food and the price of fuel it provided to Americans in Iraq, in January 2004, the firm paid back $6.7 million to the U.S. Army to cover kickbacks taken by two Halliburton employees. More investigations were underway. The company's subsidiary purchased gasoline at far-above spot prices for the U.S. in Iraq from a Kuwaiti firm close to the royal family there which, over the years, had close business ties to Marvin Bush, the president's brother. See Paul R. Krugman, "The Wars of the Texas Succession," *The New York Review of Books*, February 26, 2004.

[4] A company spokeswoman said Halliburton paid just over $15 million to the IRS for its 2002 taxes. See Bob Herbert, "The Halliburton Shuffle," *The New York Times*, January 30, 2004.

[5] The quotation was taken out of context from Benjamin Franklin's sayings. See Nicholas Kristoff, "The God Gulf," *The New York Times*, January 7, 2004.

[6] Dale Schroeder, aged 60, a property manager in Walla Walla, Washington, disagreed with Dubya's critics in 2002. He found Mr. Bush's personality appealing. "He's a down-home, folksy kind of guy that people from Walla Wall can relate to. He's not impressed with the Hollywood scene or the big-city bureaucrats. I'm so thankful we have him as president." But Mr. Schroeder expressed disappointment and surprise to learn that Enron people were among the president's main supporters. *The New York Times*, May 4, 2002.

[7] Stronger doubts existed about Warren G. Harding's role in the Teapot Dome scandal. For essays on Grant, Harding, and other presidents, including the 43rd, see Alan Brinkley and Davis Dyer, eds., *The American Presidency* (Boston: Houghton Mifflin, 2004).

[8] Who gets what if—by 2010—the 2001 tax cuts were still in place? How much extra money will taxpayers have at the end of the week thanks to the 2001 reforms? A study sponsored by the Tax Policy Center gave these answers: Persons earning $10,000 a year would wind up with an extra 98 cents per week. Taxpayers with incomes between $100,000 and $200,000 would be hit by the alternative minimum tax, which takes away most of their tax breaks. Thus, somebody earning just under $200,000 a year will have an extra $32 a week after taxes. Persons earning $200,000 or more would have 3.3% more spending money each week. At $200,000, this would mean an extra $127. However another group did even better, thanks to the child tax credit. Taxpayers earning $20,000 to $40,000 per year and who had children would end up with 4.6 to 3.7% more income—from $27 to $28 more each week. When David Cay Johnston crunched the numbers, he found that the highest-income Americans would get an increase more than six times that of the poor and nearly four times that of the affluent group just below the very rich on the income ladder. Other details in *The New York Times*, July 14, 2002.

[9] David Cay Johnston, *Perfectly Legal: The Covert Campaign to Rig Our Tax System to Benefit the Super Rich—and Cheat Everybody Else* (New York: Portfolio, 2003).

[10] The disruptions caused by outsourcing would be reduced if the U.S. government, like the Canadian, did more to provide health care and retraining, and made pensions portable.

[11] The drive to achieve, David McClelland argued, is inculcated by teaching children that industry and thrift will be rewarded—an idea completely alien to Russian folk tales and African, where Anasi the Spider Man tricks others to please his appetites and whims. See his *The Achieving Society* (New York: Irvington, 1976).

[12] The Bush administration provided small businesses a strong tax incentive to purchase vehicles weighing 6,000 pounds or more fully loaded—luxury SUVs. used by doctors and lawyers as well as pickup trucks and vans used by farmers and builders. The tax deductions allowed were a "ridiculous loophole" according to Taxpayers for Common Sense.

[13] The electricity blackout from Ohio to New York on August 14, 2003, started at a coal-burning power plant operated by First Energy, the fourth largest investor-owned energy conglomerate in the U.S. Instead of being contained, the problem led to a cascade of others. Challenged earlier about safety violations in its nuclear plant, First Energy admitted it had prioritized "production over safety." The firm faced a class-action suit in 2003 over alleged financial improprieties. Like Enron, First Energy was also audited by Arthur Andersen. Like Enron, First Energy's bosses were major contributors to Bush and to the Republican Party.

[14] See Charles Lewis, *The Buying of the President 2004: Who Really Bankrolls Bush and His Democratic Challengers—and What They Expect in Return* (New York: HarperCollins, 2004).

[15] Goldman Sachs advised buying Enron even as the company revealed the erasure of $1.2 billion in shareholder equity. The firm earned $69 million underwriting Enron. For these and other risks to American nest eggs, see: http://www.the-catbird-seat.net.

[16] "Moderate" Democrat Lieberman in early 2004 continued to defend the practice of firms giving stock options to executives, as if this were not a cost to the firm, even though this provided executives a huge incentive to jack up stock prices and then duck out—as happened with Enron. Two years after Enron imploded, the system was still broken. Clark and Dean promised to change it (Paul Krugman, "Enron and the System," *The New York Times*, January 9, 2004). Hometown boy Dick Gephardt got nearly as much beer money over the years as Dubya got Enron energy. Anheuser-Bush coughed up $518 million for the local hero while Enron generated $603 million for fellow Texan George W. Also popular locally, Lieberman collected $84 million in premiums from Hartford Financial Services. Kerry took in $230 million from a law firm where his brother practiced. The lead donor to Howard Dean was Time Warner, $65 million; to Dennis Kucinich, United Auto Workers, $54 million; to Al Sharpton, Inner City Broadcasting, $27 million. Surpassing all competitors, Shangri-La Entertainment (run by Stephen Bing, called the "playboy Democrat") gave $907 million to John Edwards! See Center for Public Integrity site: http://www.bop2004.org/bop2004.

[17] Jeffrey Toobin, "The Great Election Grab: When Does Gerrymandering Become a Threat to Democracy?" *The New Yorker*, December 8, 2003.

[18] Ron Suskind, *The Price of Loyalty: George W. Bush, The White House, and the Education of Paul O'Neill* (New York: Simon & Schuster, 2004).

[19] See the December 22, 2003 report by the Center for Budget and Policy Priorities: http://www.cbpp.org/12-22-03health-pr.htm.

[20] The U.S. tried to wipe out the sources of cocaine in South America. But America's failure to police all of Afghanistan opened the way for it to become the world's leading source of heroin.

[21] See the front-page report by Neil A. Lewis, "Bypassing Senate for Second Time, Bush Seats Judge," *The New York Times*, February 21, 2004.

[22] Ivo H. Daalder and James M. Lindsay, *America Unbound: The Bush Revolution in Foreign Policy* (Washington, D.C.: The Brookings Institution Press, 2003), p. 66.

[23] The speech writer who coined the "axis of evil" phrase later joined with the "prince of darkness" in a call for preventive and preemptive wars: David Frum and Richard Perle, *An End to Evil: How to Win the War on Terror* (New York: Random House, 2003).

[24] Bush in 2001 and Rice in 2003, quoted in Daalder and Lindsay, *America Unbound*, p. 194.

[25] www.onlinejournal.com

[26] Matthew W. L. Wald, "U.S. Calls Release of JetBlue Data Improper," *The New York Times*, February 21, 2004, p. B2.

27

Weh! Weh!
Du hast sie zerstört,
Die schöne Welt,
Mit mächtiger Faust,
Sie stürzt, sie zerfällt!
Ein Halbgott hat sie zerschlagen!
Wir tragen
Die Trümmern ins Nichts hinüber
Und klagen
Über die verlorn Schöne.

(*Faust*, lines 1607-1616)

28

Neuen Lebenslauf
Beginne
Mit hellem Sinne,
Und neue Lieder
Tönen darauf!

(*Faust*, lines 1623-1626)

29

Nur der verdient sich Freitheit wie das Leben,
Der täglich sie erobern muss.

(*Faust*, lines 11,575-11.576 and to 11,586)

Selected Readings on the George W. Bush Presidency

Abraham, Rick. *The Dirty Truth: George W. Bush's Oil and Chemical Dependency: How He Sold Out Texans and the Environment to Big Business Polluters.* Houston, TX: Mainstream Publishers, 2000.

Ali, Tariq. *Bush in Babylon: The Recolonization of Iraq.* London and New York: Verso Books, 2003.

Allman, T. D. *Rogue State: America and the World Under George W. Bush.* New York: Thunder's Mouth Press/Nation Books, 2004.

Alterman, Eric and Mark J. Green. *The Book on Bush: How George W. (Mis)leads America.* New York: Viking Press, 2004.

America's War on Terror. Eds. Patrick Hayden, Tom Lansford, and Robert P. Watson. Burlington, VT: Ashgate, 2003.

A Badly Flawed Election: Debating Bush v. Gore, the Supreme Court, and American Democracy. Ed. Ronald Dworkin. New York: New Press, 2002.

Barber, Benjamin R. *Fear's Empire: War, Terrorism, and Democracy.* New York: W. W. Norton, 2003.

Begala, Paul. *It's Still the Economy, Stupid: George W. Bush, the GOP's CEO.* New York: Simon & Schuster, 2002.

Begala, Paul. *Is Our Children Learning? The Case Against George W. Bush.* New York: Simon & Schuster, 2000.

Black, Amy E. and others. *Little Faith: the Politics of George W. Bush's Faith-based Initiatives.* Washington, D.C.: Georgetown University Press, 2004.

Boyle, Francis Anthony. *Destroying World Order: U.S. Imperialism in the Middle East Before and After September 11.* Atlanta, GA: Clarity Press, 2004.

A Blueprint for New Beginnings: A Responsible Budget for America's Priorities. Executive Office of the President of the United States. Washington, D.C.: Office of Management and Budget, Executive Office of the President: for sale by the Supt. of Docs., U.S. G.P.O., 2001. For more recent budgets, see recommended Web sites.

Brouwer, Steve, *Robbing Us Blind: The Return of the Bush Gang & the Mugging of America.* Monroe, ME: Common Courage Press, 2004.

Bruni, Frank. *Ambling Into History: The Unlikely Odyssey of George W. Bush.* New York: HarperCollins, 2002.

Bugliosi, Vincent. *The Betrayal of America: How the Supreme Court Undermined the Constitution and Chose Our President*. New York: Thunder's Mouth Press/ Nation Books, 2001.

Bush, George W. *A Charge to Keep: My Journey to the White House*. New York: Perennial, 2001.

Bush, George W. *We Will Prevail: President George W. Bush on War, Terrorism and Freedom*. New York: Continuum, 2003.

Bush v. Gore: The Question of Legitimacy. Ed. Bruce Ackerman. New Haven, CT: Yale University Press, 2002.

Bush v. Gore: The Court Cases and the Commentary. Ed. by E.J. Dionne Jr. and William Kristol. Washington, D.C.: Brookings Institution Press, 2001.

Bushisms: The Slate Book of the Accidental Wit and Wisdom of Our Forty-Third President. Ed. Jacob Weisberg. New York: Fireside, 2001.

Callinicos, Alex. *The New Mandarins of American Power: The Bush Administration's Plans for the World*. Cambridge, UK: Polity Press, 2004.

Clarke, Richard A. *Against All Enemies: Inside America's War on Terror*. New York: Free Press, 2004.

Clemens, Walter C., Jr. *America and the World, 1898-2025: Achievements, Failures, Alternative Futures*. New York: Palgrave, 2000.

Cole, David. *Enemy Aliens: Double Standards and Constitutional Freedoms in the War on Terrorism*. New York: The New Press, 2003.

Coll, Steve. *Ghost Wars: The Secret History of the CIA, Afghanistan, and Bin Laden, from the Soviet Invasion to September 10, 2001*. New York: Penguin, 2004.

Conason, Joe. *Big Lies: The Right-Wing Propaganda Machine and How It Distorts the Truth*. New York: Thomas Dunne Books, 2003.

Considering the Bush Presidency. Ed. Gary L. Gregg II and Mark J. Rozell. New York: Oxford University Press, 2004.

Corn, David. *The Lies of George W. Bush: Mastering the Politics of Deception*. New York: Crown, 2003.

Dean, John W. *Worse Than Watergate: The Secret Presidency of George W. Bush*. New York: Little, Brown, 2004.

Dershowitz, Alan M. *Supreme Injustice: How the High Court Hijacked Election 2000*. New York: Oxford University Press, 2001.

Dodge, David. *Casualty of War: The Bush Administration's Assault on the Free Press*. Amherst, NY: Prometheus, 2004.

Dover, Edwin D. *The Disputed Presidential Election of 2000: A History and Reference Guide*. Westport, CT: Greenwood Press, 2003.

Dubose, Lou, Jan Reid, and Carl M. Cannon. *Boy Genius: Karl Rove, The Brains Behind the Remarkable Political Triumph of George W. Bush*. New York: Public Affairs, 2003.

Florida 2000: A Sourcebook on the Contested Presidential Election. Ed. Mark Whitman. Boulder, CO: Lynne Rienner, 2003.

Formicola, Jo Renee, Mary C. Segers, and Paul Weber. *Faith-based Initiatives and the Bush Administration: The Good, the Bad, and the Ugly*. Lanham, MD: Rowman & Littlefield, 2003.

Franken, Al. *Lies (And the Lying Liars Who Tell Them): A Fair and Balanced Look at the Right*. New York: Dutton, 2003.

Frum, David, *The Right Man: The Surprise Presidency of George W. Bush*. New York: Random House, 2003.

Frum, David and Richard Perle. *An End to Evil: How to Win the War on Terror*. New York: Random House, 2003.

The Future is Now: America Confronts the New Genetics. Ed. William Kristol and Eric Cohen. Lanham, MD: Rowman & Littlefield, 2002.

The George W. Bush Presidency: Appraisals and Prospects. Ed. Colin Campbell and Bert A. Rockman. Washington, DC: CQ Press, 2004.

The George W. Bush Presidency: An Early Assessment. Ed. Fred I. Greenstein. Baltimore, MD: Johns Hopkins University Press, 2003.

Greene, Abner. *Understanding the 2000 Election: A Guide to the Legal Battles That Decided the Presidency*. New York: New York University Press, 2001.

Hartung, William D. *How Much Are You Making on the War, Daddy?: A Quick and Dirty Guide to War Profiteering in the Bush Administration*. New York: Thunder's Mouth Press, 2003.

Heyman, Philip B. *Terrorism, Freedom, and Security: Winning Without War.* Cambridge, MA: The MIT Press, 2003.

High Risk and Big Ambition: The Presidency of George W. Bush. Ed. Steven E. Schier. Pittsburgh, PA: University of Pittsburgh Press, 2004.

Hightower, Jim. *Thieves in High Places: They've Stolen Our Country and It's Time to Take It Back.* New York: Viking Press, 2003.

Hintoff, Nat. *The War on the Bill of Rights.* New York: Seven Stories Press, 2003.

Huberman, Jack. *The Bush-Hater's Handbook: A Guide to the Most Appalling Presidency in the Past 100 Years.* New York: Nation Books, 2003.

Ide, Arthur Frederick. *George W. Bush: Portrait of a Compassionate Conservative.* Las Colinas, TX: Monument Press, 2000.

Ivins, Molly and Lou Dubose. *Bushwhacked: Life in George W. Bush's America.* New York: Random House, 2003.

Ivins, Molly and Lou Dubose. *Shrub: The Short But Happy Political Life of George W. Bush.* New York: Random House, 2000.

Jarvis, Robert M., and others. *Bush v. Gore: The Fight for Florida's Vote.* New York: Kluwer Law International, 2001.

Kagan, Robert. *Of Paradise and Power: America and Europe in the New World Order.* New York: Alfred A. Knopf, 2003.

Kaplan, David A. *The Accidental President: How 413 lawyers, 9 Supreme Court Justices, and 5,963,110 (give or take a few) Floridians Landed George W. Bush in the White House.* New York: William Morrow, 2001.

Kaplan, Lawrence and William Kristol. *The War Over Iraq: Saddam's Tyranny and America's Mission.* San Francisco, CA: Encounter Books, 2003.

Kellner, Douglas. *From 9/11 to Terror War: The Dangers of the Bush Legacy.* Lanham, MD: Rowman & Littlefield, 2003.

Kettl, Donald F. *Team Bush: Leadership Lessons from the Bush White House.* New York: McGraw-Hill, 2003.

Krames, Jeffrey A. *The Rumsfeld Way: The Leadership Wisdom of a Battle-Hardened Maverick.* New York: McGraw-Hill Trade, 2002.

Krugman, Paul. *The Great Unraveling: Losing Our Way in the New Century*. New York: W.W. Norton & Company, 2003.

Landau, Saul. *The Pre-Emptive Empire: A Guide to Bush's Kingdom*. Sterling, VA: Pluto Press, 2003.

Lewis, Charles. *The Buying of the President 2004 : Who's Really Bankrolling Bush and His Democratic Challengers—and What They Expect in Return*. New York: Perennial, 2004.

Lind, Michael. *Made in Texas: George W. Bush and the Southern Takeover of American Politics*. New York: Basic Books, 2003.

Loconte, Joe. *God, Government and the Good Samaritan: The Promise and the Peril of the President's Faith Based Agenda*. Washington, D.C.: Heritage Foundation, 2001.

Lord, Carnes. *The Modern Prince: What Leaders Need to Know Now*. New Haven, CT: Yale University Press, 2003.

Lost Liberties: Ashcroft and the Assault on Personal Freedom. Ed. Cynhia Brown. New York: The New Press, 2003.

Mann, Jim and James. *Rise of the Vulcans: The History of Bush's War Cabinet*. New York: Viking, 2004.

Mansfield, Stephen. *The Faith of George W. Bush*. Lake Mary, FL: Charisma House, 2003.

Miller, Mark Crispin. *The Bush Dyslexicon: Observations on a National Disorder*. New York: W.W. Norton, 2001.

Miller, Mark Crispin. *Cruel and Unusual: the Case Against Bush, Cheney, and the Media*. New York: W.W. Norton & Company, 2004.

Mitchell, Elizabeth, W. *Revenge of the Bush Dynasty*. New York: Hyperion, 2000.

Moore, James and Slater Wayne. *Bush's Brain: How Karl Rove Made George W. Bush Presidential*. New York: Wiley, 2003.

Moore, Michael. *Dude, Where's My Country?* New York: Warner Books, 2003.

Moore, Michael. *Fahrenheit 9/11* [film, 2004].

Moore, Michael. *Stupid White Men—and Other Sorry Excuses for the State of the Nation*. New York: ReganBooks, 2001.

Newhouse, John. *Imperial America: The Bush Assault on the World Order*. New York: Knopf, 2003.

Palast, Greg. *The Best Democracy Money Can Buy: An Investigative Reporter Exposes the Truth about Globalization, Corporate Cons, and High Finance Fraudsters*. New York: Plume, 2003.

Palast, Greg and others. *Democracy and Regulation: How the Public Can Govern Essential Services*. Sterling, VA.: Pluto Press, 2003.

Parenti, Christian. *The Soft Cage: Surveillance in America From Slavery to the War on Terror*. New York: Basic Books, 2003.

Phillips, Kevin P. *American Dynasty: Aristocracy, Fortune, and the Politics of Deceit in the House of Bush*. New York: Viking, 2004.

Post, Jerrold M. *Leaders and Their Followers in a Dangerous World: The Psychology of Political Behavior*. Ithaca, NY: Cornell University Press, 2004.

Present Dangers: Crisis and Opportunity in American Foreign and Defense Policy. Ed. Robert Kagan and William Kristol. San Francisco, CA: Encounter Books, 2000.

Presidential (Mis)Speak: The Very Curious Language of George W. Bush (Volumes 1 & 2). Ed. Robert S. Brown. Skaneateles, NY: Outland, 2003.

Rampton, Sheldon and John Stauber. *Weapons of Mass Deception: The Uses of Propaganda in Bush's War on Iraq*. New York: Jeremy P. Tarcher/Penguin, 2003.

Riddell, Peter. *The Odd Couple: Tony Blair's Love Affair with George W. Bush and America*. London: Politico's, 2003.

Ritter, Scott. *Frontier Justice: Weapons of Mass Destruction and the Bushwhacking of America*. New York: Context Books, 2003.

Rosen, Jeffrey. *The Naked Crowd: Reclaiming Security and Freedom*. New York: Random House, 2004.

Silverstein, Michael, *Talking Politics: The Substance of Style From Abe to "W"*. Chicago: Prickly Paradigm Press, 2003.

Schweizer, Peter and Rochelle. *The Bushes: Portrait of a Dynasty*. New York: Doubleday, 2004.

Soros, George. *The Bubble of American Supremacy: Correcting the Misuse of American Power*. New York: Public Affairs, 2004.

Sperry, Paul E. *Crude Politics: How Bush's Oil Cronies Hijacked the War on Terrorism*. Nashville, TN: WND Books, 2003.

Stevens, Stuart. *The Big Enchilada: Campaign Adventures With the Cockeyed Optimists From Texas Who Won the Biggest Prize in Politics*. New York: Free Press, 2001.

Still More George W. Bushisms: Neither in French, nor in English, nor in Mexican. Ed. Jacob Weisberg. New York: Simon & Schuster, 2003.

Suskind, Ron. *The Price of Loyalty: George W. Bush, the White House, and the Education of Paul O'Neill*. New York: Simon & Schuster, 2004.

Taught to Lead: The Education of the Presidents of the United States. Ed. Fred L. Philadelphia: Mason Crest Publishers, 2004.

Thompson, Carolyn B. and James W. Ware. *The Leadership Genius of George W. Bush: 10 Commonsense Lessons From the Commander in Chief*. New York: Wiley, 2003.

Unger, Craig. *House of Bush, House of Saud: The Secret Relationship Between the World's Two Most Powerful Dynasties*. New York: Scribner, 2004.

Vidal, Gore. *Dreaming War: Blood for Oil and the Cheney-Bush Junta*. New York: Thunder's Mouth Press, 2002.

The Vote: Bush, Gore, and the Supreme Court. Ed. Cass R. Sunstein and Richard A. Epstein. Chicago: University of Chicago Press, 2001.

Waldman, Paul. *Fraud: The Strategy Behind the Bush Lies and Why the Media Didn't Tell You*. Naperville, IL: Sourcebooks Trade, 2004.

The War on Our Freedoms: Civil Liberties in an Age of Terrorism. Ed. Richard C. Leone and Greg Anrig, Jr. New York: Public Affairs, 2003.

The White House World: Transitions, Organization, and Office Operations. Ed. Martha Joynt Kumar and Terry Sullivan. College Station, TX: Texas A&M University Press, 2003.

Wilson, Joseph. *The Politics of Truth: Inside the Lies that Led to War and Betrayed My Wife's CIA Identity, A Diplomat's Memoir*. New York: Carrroll & Graft, 2004.

Woodward, Bob. *Bush at War*. New York: Simon & Schuster, 2002.

Woodward, Bob. *Plan of Attack*. New York: Simon & Schuster, 2004.

Zelnick, Robert, *Winning Florida: How the Bush Team Fought the Battle*. Stanford, CA: Hoover Institution, 2001.

Web Sites on the George W. Bush Presidency

GOVERNMENT SITES

http://www.whitehouse.gov/president/
The President's official website

http://www.whitehouse.gov/omb/budget/fy2005
Budget of the United States Government, Fiscal Year 2005.

http://www.cbo.gov/
Congressional Budget Office

http://www.whitehouse.gov/nsc/nss.html
The National Security Strategy of the United States of America [September 17, 2002].

http://www.defenselink.mil/execsec/adr2003
Rumsfeld, Donald H., Secretary of Defense. Annual Report to the President and the Congress 2003

BUSH-CHENEY CAMPAIGN SITES

Bush-Cheney [computer file], Austin, TX: Bush for President, 2000, available at the Library of Congress

http://www.georgewbush.com/
partisan coverage

http://www.georgewbush.com/Blog/
partisan report on the president's activities

http://www.politics1.com/bush.htm
pro-Bush site with index of other sites

UNOFFICIAL SITES

http://www.theamericanenterprise.org/
research and analysis at the American Enterprise Institute (conservative)

http://ap.grolier.com/
uses material from five Grolier encyclopedias to look at presidents and presidential elections past and present

http://www.brookings.edu/default.htm
research and analysis at the Brookings Institution (liberal)

http://www.bushwatch.org/
exposés of the president, e.g., his reserve service record

www.commondreams.org
progressive news and views

http://www.c-span.org/homepage.asp?Cat=Current_Event&Code=Bush_Admin
C-SPAN news on the Bush administration

http://www.democrats.com/
independent, "patriotic progressive" Democrats

http://www.thedubyareport.com/
comprehensive and critical, with links to published and electronic media

http://www.fas.org
analysis of political and security issues from a science perspective

http://www.fnsg.com/
Federal News Service, a private organization, provides transcripts from government speeches, hearings, etc.

http://www.globalsecurity.com
analysis of security and UN affairs

http://www.heritage.org/
policy and analysis by the Heritage Foundation (conservative)

http://www.inthesetimes.com/
In These Times magazine

http://www.iraqbodycount.net/
estimated toll of coalition forces and Iraqis

http://www.thememoryhole.org/
documents and photos we are not supposed to see—from records of Governor Bush in Texas and noise ratings of snowmobiles in Yellowstone to tortured Iraqi prisoners and mortuary procedures at Dover Air Force Base

http://www.motherjones.com/news/blog/
critical analysis in a progressive magazine

http://www.onlinejournal.com/
tries to provide news not found in mainstream media

http://www.realchange.org/bushjr.htm
Skeleton closet—"all the dirt on all the candidates"

http://www.publicintegrity.org/dtaweb/home.asp
nonpartisan Center for Public Integrity

http://www.salon.com/
sophisticated analysis of politics, business, and IT

http://www.tompaine.com/
"public interest journal" with articles by Robert Reich, James Carroll, David Corn

http://www.thetruthaboutgeorge.com/
news about Bush policies toward women and other groups at risk from the National
Organization for Women

http://www.votetoimpeach.org/
initiated by Ramsey Clark, former Attorney General of the United States

http://www.wage-slave.org/scorecard.html
"Scoreboard of evil"